MW00427182

The Language of Heaven

5 Gifts That Create Legacy

PAT GANO

AUTHOR ACADEMY elite

Copyright 2017 © by Pat Gano

All rights reserved. No part of this publication may be reproduced, distributed, or transmitted in any form or by any means, including photocopying, recording, or other electronic or mechanical methods, without the prior written permission of the publisher, except in the case of brief quotations embodied in critical reviews and certain other noncommercial uses permitted by copyright law.

Unless noted, all Bible quotations are from the Message Bible. The Bible in Contemporary Language was created and translated by Eugene H. Peterson and published in segments from 1993 to 2002 ©. It is an idiomatic translation of the original languages of the Bible.

Printed in the United States of America
2017 First Edition

Subjet Index:
Gano, Pat
Title: Language of Heaven: 5 Gifts That Create Legacy

ISBN-13: 978-1640851177
ISBN-10: 1640851178
LCCN: 2017914422

Author Academy Elite
Powell, Ohio

To protect the privacy of individuals some names
have been changed.

Endorsements

This book will speak to you in many ways as you not only learn more about God but learn how to enter a deeper relationship with Him you might otherwise only hope for. Pat Gano's insights come directly from her own walk and are blended with years of careful study. While many have been blessed to receive her teachings in person now this great book will allow you and countless others to be equipped to live a life of true success and significance. To know Pat is to love her and any moments with her make you want more! Read this in a place where you can "take it all in". You will be glad you did . . . forever!

Scott M Fay,
Entrepreneur, Author and Speaker

Pat Gano says she asked God for the gift of how she would look walking on earth as it is in heaven. Anyone who knows Pat knows that she is one of many gifts God has blessed us with on this earth. As a loving and humble servant of God, she generously shares her wisdom and brings this gift to life through this soon to be enduring classic, Language of Heaven. It's easy to fall into the day-to-day rigors of life and quickly lose our way, our identity, and our purpose. Take a step back, be blessed, and allow yourself to be drawn into the story of Bernice as she surrenders all circumstances around her to God and embraces a new destiny. And "listen" as God speaks directly to you through the words and wisdom Pat blesses us with. Pat, thank you for this gift!

Joel Kessel
Owner of Kessel Communications, LLC, and creator of the "Your Media Strategy" an online program for authors, entrepreneurs and leaders of small businesses and organizations. Joel@Kesselcommunications.com

I was on a master-class-teaching call with Paul Martinelli, President of the John Maxwell Team, when I heard a fellow participant's voice – a lady – describe how she asks God direct questions. She described how she writes them down in black ink, then waits for HIS answer. She said there are times HE doesn't answer her—at least not right away—but often times, HE does answer; then she records HIS answers in red ink. My heart leaped inside me and I thought, I must talk with this lady!

Initially, I didn't catch her name, but on a subsequent call, I heard her speak again and we connected. This connection has become one of the greatest blessings of my life. Why? I find Pat Gano extraordinary in so many ways; particularly in her intimate relationship with God. She intentionally walks closely with HIM daily . . . talks with HIM and shares HIM with others—as though HE is standing right there! Having read the manuscript, I have no doubt this work is divinely inspired. It is pure gold delivered directly from the heart of God through HIS servant, "Blessing".

Dorothy Guy Bonvillain, PhD.
Leadership Coach and Author of Loving Your Life:
7 Steps for Military Wives.

Through God, Pat's words have always been encouraging, enlightening and edifying to me. The "Language of Heaven" has captured the communion between God and His child, as she hears from the Lord and speaks to the Lord. Pat you are a BLESSING to me. Thank you for your friendship and your obedience to write this book.

Pastor Rudy Diaz Jr.
San Diego, California

I can't think of a person more qualified to write about the language of heaven besides Pat. Her unique and personal relationship with God will flow to you with every turn of the page. Pat shares truths that have the power to transform your relationship with God or introduce Him to you for the first time. If you ever wanted to spend sometime with a disciple on earth, this book is for you.

Wendy Taylor
President
Freedom Trade International
www.freedomtradeinternational.org

I first met Pat Gano at the John Maxwell International Certification three years ago. I immediately knew that she was someone I would want in my inner circle. At times, being around Miss Pat is like being around someone who speaks a different language. I find myself intrigued, listening closely, and hanging on every word she says. In fact, I have come to realize that Miss Pat does, indeed, speak another language . . . *The Language of Heaven*! Words that come out of her mouth, I believe, are anointed. Miss Pat is a treasure. At 83 years old, she continues to invest in her own personal growth and in sharing all that she has learned from her rich years on earth to as many people as she can to ensure they all get to see the glory of heaven. Bless yourself and join me in reading the "Language of Heaven, and you will learn to speak with the authority of Heaven."

Melanie Massey
Entrepreneur, Artist, Physical Therapist
CEO Melanie Massey Physical Therapy
CEO MoCo Leadership
Owner/Artist at Mojoy

The Language of Heaven is a beautiful, life-changing book that will leave you longing to live a life that is Heaven on Earth! You will see a precious relationship unfold between God the Father, Jesus, the Holy Spirit and a girl named Bernice. The dialogue is powerful! It is truly and honor to read a book written by an 83-year-old woman! Her perspective and wisdom is so refreshing. It will revolutionize your thinking. So grab your coffee or tea and sit down to read a book where the scripture 1 Titus 2:3-5 comes alive! . . . Let the older women teach the younger women.

Erica Foster
Entrepreneur, Coach, and Speaker
Author of "You Taught My Feet To Dance: Learning to Follow His Lead"
www.ericamariefoster.com

Pat Gano is a true inspiration! While most people in their 80's are looking backwards and reminiscing on "the good ol' days," Pat is looking forward to the impact she is called by God to make in her lifetime. She has no plans to slow down and rest on her laurels. Instead, she is passionate about freeing souls to soar. If you want a role model to make the most of your "golden years," Pat is your gal! Take to heart her words and wisdom. God is using Pat in an incredible way in her generation.

Chris McClure
Coach & Leadership Trainer, Lead Life BIG—
www.LeadLifeBIG.com
Co-Founder, GROWING Maximized Leaders—
www.GrowingMaximizedLeaders.com

This book is dedicated to:

My Father God, Jesus, and Holy Spirit . . . I am humbly honored and deeply thankful that you are my Creator. You saved my soul, and you are my beloved bridegroom. I am seeking to live Heaven on earth because of You.

Pete, my Divine Soul Mate . . . you are the wind beneath my wings. I couldn't have written this book without you.

Beth, my precious daughter . . . you and your loving family give me my forever joy.

Andrew, my amazing son . . . my continuous joy flows from you and your beautiful family.

Contents

Foreword

At the age of seventy, Pat Gano dramatically reexperienced JESUS. She spoke to Him directly, and her conversation went something like this: "Jesus, your disciples asked You how to pray, and You taught them 'Thy will be done on earth as it is in HEAVEN.' As I look around, I don't see anyone, not even people in church, walking on earth as it is in heaven. Would You be so kind as to give me the gift of how I would look walking on earth as it is in heaven, Will you give me that gift?"

Seven years ago, GOD told her He would write a book using her. It was to be a road map to GOD for her descendants for a thousand generations forward, or until He sends HIS SON JESUS back to earth. The book would also be for those who have ears to hear and eyes to see.

This unique book is a direct result of conversations Pat has had with GOD over the past thirteen years. It is not like any other book you have ever read, for GOD graciously and generously wrote the book through Pat. Except for the mistakes, she declares that she can take no credit for this book.

Pat has counseled women most of her adult life. In this book, she has used some of the most tragic, but real stories from real people as a foundation for a fictional character named 'Bernice' who reaches out in desperation to GOD.

GOD'S pure, holy, and heavenly love responds by giving 'Bernice' a new identity. GOD calls her "Blessing." He tells her that she is blessed in order to bless others.

Through dialogue with the Father God, Jesus, and Holy Spirit, Blessing is invited into intimacy with GOD. She learns to surrender totally all of her circumstances and all within her to GOD. She learns the purpose of why she was born.

Blessing walks out her destiny to leave a Godly inheritance. God gives her a life of significant impact on the world. Moreover, heaven is more heavily populated because people are drawn to GOD as a result of 'Blessings' example of walking in humility, surrender, giving and receiving. As you read and practice exchanging Blessing's name and story for your name and story, you— like she—will experience GOD speaking, personally, gently, and lovingly into your life and circumstances.

This unique book will become an enduring classic for both you and your descendants.

Kary Oberbrunner, author of *Elixir Project, Day Job To Dream Job, The Deeper Path* and *Your Secret Name*

Cast of Characters

GODHEAD – FATHER GOD, JESUS, HOLY SPIRIT

BERNICE — Bernice, a fictional character whose life story is a combination of many tragic, but real stories of real women

BLESSING — Bernice receives JESUS as God's Gift to her, and God changes her name to Blessing

We — Godhead

Us — Godhead

Our — Godhead

Satan — the enemy of all

Introduction

Suddenly, my world changed when I turned 70 years old, while reading Matthew 5 in the Bible. JESUS taught His disciples to pray like this:

"Our FATHER in heaven, hallowed be Thy Name.
Your Kingdom come, Your will be done on earth as it is in heaven".

I paused and began to speak to JESUS.
Not sure where I was going with this, I simply said:

"JESUS, this is how You taught your disciples to pray. As I look around me, Your people are not living on earth moment by moment concentrating on doing what the FATHER is doing and saying what He is saying.

How do we do that? How do we obey You?

JESUS, I am seventy years old, so I can't have too many more years left. For the rest of my life would You be so kind as to give me the gift of showing me 'How would Pat live on earth as it is in heaven?' I have no language for that."

The thirteen years since then have been the most *glorious* and the *hardest* years of my life.

Strangely, GOD has given me *a whole new way of thinking* about life. Everything has been turned upside down. Now when I am tested, when I have a trial, when trouble comes, or even when I experience sickness, *I celebrate that I get to know GOD in a way that I never could have known Him had this never come into my life.*

Celebrating those challenges in my life is now a taste of heaven for me. It certainly is not how we typically respond to these things on earth. It truly has to be a new experience of GOD's Presence in me. Thirteen years later, He is still answering this prayer I prayed when I turned 70.

One night, seven years ago, I was startled awake and sat straight up in bed. It was the first time GOD spoke to me in this way, and as with the heroes of our faith, fear gripped my heart. He said words I will never forget: *"Do not fear! I am giving you an assignment. Before you die, I want you to write a book and start a non-profit* (which remains imprecise). The book will be a "roadmap" to Me for your descendants for a thousand years forward or until My Son returns. Yes, it will also be a "roadmap" to Me for those who have ears to hear and eyes to see."

2

Introduction

I became a "Listener". Here in Columbus, Ohio, 2017, GOD gave me the name of this book and *the five part road map* to FATHER, JESUS and HOLY SPIRIT which *creates His Legacy* in each one of us. I take no credit for anything but the mistakes in this book. He wrote it by speaking to me through many of you who have messaged me on different days scriptures, stories, sermons, etc. that exactly matched where I was writing in the book. Both GOD and I thank you for your faithfulness! With this happening as I wrote the book, I had so much fun just watching where He was working and joining Him there.

As I have found, so I hope you will find the words of this book to be a spiritual stimulus to make FATHER GOD, JESUS, and HOLY SPIRIT your *First Love!*

This book is divided into a Five Part Roadmap . . .

Part 1, <u>*INTIMACY:*</u> Nearness to GOD and confidence in Him changes everything!

Part 2, <u>*IDENTITY:*</u> You are who GOD says you are . . . nothing more, nothing less!

Part 3, <u>*INTENT:*</u> Joy is found by walking in the purpose GOD created you to fulfill!

Part 4, <u>*INHERITANCE:*</u> GOD makes His deposit through you into generations who follow you!

Part 5, <u>*IMPACT:*</u> Humbly surrender, give, receive, impact the World, and populate Heaven!

The book opens as a dialogue and continues as a dialogue. It is written in a conversational script format between a female named *Bernice* (which means "*bringer of victory*"), *GOD as FATHER, GOD as JESUS His Son, GOD as HOLY SPIRIT*, and *satan*. I have counseled women most of my adult life, and Bernice is a fictional character whose life story combines tragic, but real stories of real women who have been a part of my life. These make up Bernice's story.

In Part 1: *INTIMACY*, Bernice converses with GOD and accepts CHRIST

In Part 2: *IDENTITY*, GOD tells her the name He has written on her white stone in heaven (Revelation 2:17). You, too, can ask Him what is written on your white stone. After her name is revealed, *Bernice is called "Blessing"* for the remainder of the book.

To get the most out of reading this book, I suggest that *when Bernice speaks; replace her name with your name.* When Bernice tells *her story*, replace it with *your story. May the beauty of reading this book with your name and your story make it possible for you to hear GOD, JESUS and HOLY SPIRIT speak directly to you.*

May His Word transform your life into a life filled with His Glory,

Pat Gano
September 1, 2017

Part One

INTIMACY

"That the GOD of our Lord JESUS CHRIST,
the FATHER of glory, may give to you the spirit
of wisdom
and revelation in the knowledge of Him."

BERNICE speaking to GOD

GOD, You don't understand. I can't come to You. I am too dirty. At times, I have not even believed You exist. I've tried to figure out how to live in a world . . . where a daddy called his daughter the curse of the family, where a daddy beats his children, where a daddy rapes his daughters and teaches his son to steal, where I abort my son, where I give a little girl away never to see her again, where my mom sold me to the men that came to see her, where a little girl was told she was worthless, trash, stupid, useless, and a dumb dog. They shamed me and blamed me. It was so scary. I was terrified. I was alone.

I blamed You, GOD. I got to college, pretended to be an intellectual, studied philosophy, and decided to live like an epicurean. What a mess! My anger just grew like a weed. I put on a shroud—a mask upon a mask to keep others away. I was emotionally shut down, acting like a stoic. Nothing could touch me. I thought I was thinking, but I never knew who I really was. I was a phony who foolishly thought I was powerful enough to figure out my life by myself. How wrong I was! I was lost! I looked to people for answers to find peace, purpose and understanding. It never worked!

Deeper and deeper, I delved into eastern religion—even practicing kundalini yoga, table-tipping, using spirit guides, and studying the occult—all of it held my interest. All my training to do group therapy to help others was based on knowledge that comes from man. What a joke! People "found themselves", but then decided their spouses weren't as "evolved" as they were. They divorced and remarried. In their quest for answers, the cycle repeated over and over. I couldn't live with their pain on top of my pain. So You see, I can't take much more GOD. I have tried everything but You. I have tried everything to find peace and to find how to live in this world of deep pain, prejudice, hopelessness, and despair.

GOD as FATHER speaking to BERNICE

My beloved, I have been waiting for you. I AM Your good, good Abba FATHER. I want to adopt you into My Family as My Child. Your enemy satan has lied to you all these years because he knows how to exploit your weaknesses and intimidate you by pointing out your faults. He lies with half-truths. He corrupts your thinking by using your faults and mistakes to prove to you that there is no GOD—that even if I existed, you would not qualify.

satan speaking to BERNICE

Don't listen to Him, Bernice. Face the facts—you aren't good enough to be in this righteous and holy crowd. So, The Bible does say that GOD chose you and will make you righteous and holy—big deal! You know, and I know, you do some really horrendous things. You've tried that self-improvement crap. If you are really thinking seriously about this GOD, don't you think you ought to clean yourself up a bit before you even consider talking to Him.

GOD speaking to BERNICE

My beloved, you have a choice. Listen to ME to find real life, or, continue to listen to satan to find real death.

BERNICE speaking to GOD

Everything and everyone else I have tried didn't work. I might as well give listening to You a try, GOD. It's obvious people generally don't care and "no one who said they did" did much for me. I have nowhere else to go . . .

GOD as FATHER speaking to BERNICE

Bernice, this is the real you I have been waiting for your whole life long—you with all masks off! Welcome Home! I will celebrate your homecoming with a party! My beloved, every single one of your bad deeds is covered by My Love for you. Because you have opened the way for Me to prove Myself to you, I will make you completely new by the power of the HOLY SPIRIT of My Son JESUS! His Blood shed on the cross covers the result of everything that has been done to you, and the result of every destructive thing you have ever done, which disregarded Me. You now can choose to be a part of My Royal Family!

BERNICE speaking to GOD as FATHER

Wait a minute GOD. I've heard words like these somewhere once before. What do You mean I will *be* a new person by the blood of JESUS CHRIST? That sounds weird to me.

GOD as FATHER speaking to BERNICE

Yes, My beloved, this must sound unusual to you. Trust me dear one. Listen with your heart, not your mind. JESUS is My Son. I sent Him to earth for many reasons. I sent Him to be an example to show everyone, including you, how to really live and love rather than to settle for the kind of the life you have survived. For this reason, My Son died in your place on a cross, and His Blood was shed to cover all bad things done to you and all bad things done by you— past, present, and future. JESUS, My Son has done this for everyone.

You choose to come to Us from the kingdom of darkness which is run by your enemy satan whose intent is to steal, kill and destroy you (John 10:10). We bring you unstoppable abundant Life that flows without ceasing. You have chosen to come Home to Us.

We love you so much that We invite you to be a part of Our Family and live forever with Us. No one has ever loved you as much as We love you. We hold you securely in safe arms. We sent Our HOLY SPIRIT to you on earth to bring you to Our celebration of your homecoming. We wash away your tears. We pour the pure life-giving water of Our Presence over you and into you. You recline in the refreshing waters of Our Love. Let the renewing waters of Our HOLY SPIRIT wash away all loss, all pain, all prejudice, all helplessness, all hopelessness. All the rejection you have experienced that brings tears through the night to your pillow and all fear that swims inside your mind will be washed away.

BERNICE speaking to GOD as FATHER

But You don't understand, if I let them see my lies, see the real me, see this carrier of lack, see this imposter of a dozen masks, they will run!

GOD as FATHER speaking to BERNICE

No, My beloved. Let me explain some things: I am inviting you into your new life, into the new you that I created you to become before the world was formed (Psalm 139:16). We will wash all of your old life off of you. Yes, your old habits will be broken, your self-limiting beliefs will be changed, and you will believe My Truth which you opposed. You will be a new creation (2 Corinthians 5:17). You have come home. Your old self will die on the cross with My Son. I will place a majestic robe of My Peace around you, over you, and under you. When you ask My Son to live in you, My Son will stay for eternity and you will rest in the center of My Son forever. You will be adopted into Our Royal Family. You will be My Child on earth as you will be in heaven. You are meant to only do what I am doing and only say what I am saying just like My Son did when He was on earth (John 5:19).

This may seem to be a little advanced for you right now, but no worry, My HOLY SPIRIT will teach you. I am inviting you to ask My Son into your heart—the core and essence of who you are, into every molecule and element of your life. The result will be: you will become a new creation; the old version of you will be dead. My Son not only died on the cross for your sins, He died on the cross as you and your sin (2 Corinthians 5:21). So, your past will die with Him, you will be buried with Him, you will be raised brand new with Him, and you will be seated in Him in heaven (Ephesians 2:6). He will be in you and live in you; you will be in Us and live in Us (John 14:20). I will place you in the center of My Son in heaven next to My Throne, so that the HOLY SPIRIT will teach you how you are created in Our Image, created for relationship with Us. Love Us not just with your head, but also with your heart, with your whole being, with all that is you (Luke 10:27)!

When you ask My Son into your heart, He "comes to stay" in you—He is in you, and you are in Him. I gave you a wonderful imagination! So, imagine yourself walking on earth in the center of My Son with the high Strong Tower full-protection of His Presence surrounding you on every side. Imagine within that high Strong Tower around you is everything that is My Son: His Name, His Blood, His Resurrection Power, His Joy, His Kindness, His Peace, His Hope, His Longsuffering, His Majesty, His Love, His Light, His Wisdom, His Understanding, His Knowledge, His Counsel, His Protection, and His plan for your life (Proverbs 18:10). Now, imagine His strong High Tower Presence has unending access open all the way up to Our Thrones in heaven.

You will live in the Holy Spirit in and above your circumstances. No demon, no evil, no judgment, no rejection, no financial trouble, no job, no rebellious children, no inability to conceive a child, no spouse, no divorce, no *destructive negative* comes toward you without full contact with My Son's Presence. There they must fall! After you invite My Son into you, I want you to be aware every moment as you walk on earth that you have unending open direct access to Our Thrones in heaven. Our Love flows down like warm liquid gold from Our Throne into the full protection of the Presence of My Son that totally surrounds you. You will live, hidden in the center of My Son (Isaiah 46:8-11, John 14:20).

My Child, We will continue to teach you to always rest, abide, celebrate, and walk in gratitude!

Thank Me that the blood of My Son shuts down the enemy, his fallen angels, and his plan for your life! We will teach you how to take authority over the enemy. When the enemy tries to take you down, just remember he is just a big bully who only wins when you believe his lies that are designed to limit you. Learn to just stand confidently in the high Strong Tower Presence! In the authority of Jesus, you can command satan to leave, and he must respond to Jesus alive in you! WE are with you. We will never leave you. We want yours to be a glorious victorious life no matter what circumstances come your way!

You are at the door. You have just come home, and we are all still celebrating, excited about the new life you are about to discover. I see your future made new: knowing the *intimacy* of who We are for you, acting in your new *identity* in Christ, *implementing* your purpose, enjoying your godly *inheritance*, satisfied by your godly *impact* which increases the population of heaven! Joyfully you will learn daily moment by moment to surrender—spirit, soul and body. Beloved, you have a life of significance ahead of you. My Child, you will live in abundance with Me forever!

Invite My Son to come to you now. Ask My Son into your heart, into your being, into everything that is you, Bernice . . .

BERNICE speaking to GOD as FATHER

Oh FATHER, I don't deserve to be Your child. I have done so many wrong things against You and other people. I am a mess. My own mother hated me. My father abandoned me. I am worthless. I am hopeless. You don't understand how I hate so many people. So many people have hurt me. I can't forgive them!

GOD as FATHER speaking to BERNICE

My beloved child, you give Me such honor when you tell Me the truth. What you have just said about yourself is 100% true. What you said about Me, that "I don't understand", is 100% false. I 100% understand you. But, understand this: I cannot forgive you if you do not forgive them, and I have the 100% solution for your inability to forgive. Let's work together on the assignment I have for you.

1. Choose one person that you now believe you cannot forgive.
2. Bring that person to Me for the next seven days and ask Me to bless them in every way. At first, you will experience the struggle with not wanting to do this challenging assignment. I do not ask you to forget what was done to you. I ask you to

allow Me to exchange your heart for My Heart toward that person. I want you to understand that you are poisoning yourself with bitterness you feel toward that person. *My precious Child, come to Me. Learn to trust Me, and I will take care of it for you.*

3. In these seven days, imagine yourself asking Me to bless, change, and improve this person's spirit, mind, emotions, body, will, relationships, job, marriage, and family. Then, ask Me to do for you and for that person what only I can do!

4. After seven days, you will know We have changed your heart because you are made in Our Image. When you invite My Son JESUS into everything that is you Bernice, you will be a new creation. Your old self will be nailed to the cross. You will still notice bad habits that must go—but more and more you will want them gone. But keep your eyes, mind and heart celebrating your new creation, your new identity, and focus on JESUS. You will begin to experience the joy of being transformed. Read the Gospels (Matthew, Mark, Luke, John) in the Bible, carefully over and over again, following the example of how My Son, JESUS lived on earth. These books will show you how My Son walked on earth, and this is the model for how you will begin to walk on earth. Take notice of the time when you come to the place where you say "FATHER, I simply choose to forgive _____."

My HOLY SPIRIT will teach you who *We* are and who *you* are in Christ. HOLY SPIRIT will comfort you and will convict you of what is right and where you are wrong. He will make Our Image clear to you and guide you to focus on how you will benefit when you surrender your will, exchange your thinking for His thoughts, and then allow Him to act through you. You will learn about Our Kingdom and the resources that become yours when you are Mine. HOLY SPIRIT will teach you as you invest your time in knowing what I've said and become familiar with My Voice through My Word (the Bible), invest in getting to know Me in worship, invest your mind in being with, and taught by people who know Me personally. And yes, even your circumstances will draw you to Us, and He will show you how sweet intimate relationship with Us [The Godhead] can be! We will be your family!

Even if it seems a little silly, trust ME on this one. Open your left hand, and put it out in front of you. Now, open your right hand, and put it close to but not touching the left hand. The left hand represents the giants—negative circumstances, sickness, and conflicts that come your way. Your right hand represents the exact opposite of what your left hand represents. Your right hand represents Me. Looking at both hands opened, close, but not touching, You will see I am always there with you, no matter how deep your point of pain. The exact opposite of what pain is in your left hand is in your right hand—Me. I want you to realize you are in a battle. You have two choices. You can focus on your giant negative circumstance, or choose Me.

When a test, trial, trouble, or sickness comes your way, it does not belong to you. It is mine. When negative things happen, stop. I want you to come to Me. I want you to praise Me, worship Me, and thank

Me that you are getting a spiritual upgrade from My HOLY SPIRIT to the degree this "bad thing" has come against you. Celebrate inside—let your heart leap for joy! What seems bad is good because, when you and I work together, I will surely give back more than seven times what the thieving enemy seeks to steal from you (Proverbs 6:31, John 10:10).

Instead of focusing on negative circumstances, I want you to focus on these four questions:

1. GOD, what part of Your Nature are You teaching me to live out on earth today that I could learn no other way than through this fight?
2. GOD, what are your Promises to me in this fight?
3. GOD, what are your Provisions for me in this fight?
4. GOD, how can I bring glory to You in this fight?

My beloved, this is how My HOLY SPIRIT trains you to remain in Our Image as you were created to live. The same Holy Spirit that was *upon* Caleb and Joshua is *within* you (Numbers 14:24, Numbers 27:18) and you will have your own version of your shared story. I trust you enough to let you face your giant with the warrior nature of My Holy Spirit Who always wins (Zechariah 4:6)!

When you invite My Son into *everything that is you*, He is in *you*, and *You* are in Him. You are One. He defeated your enemy satan 2,000+ years ago. When you see yourself this way, you will remember you carry a *new Spirit* into every single one of your circumstances. You will remember that you have all of heaven in the battle with you. You will see your circumstances as We see them! We love a good fight because in Us you always win (Exodus 14:13, 2 Chronicles 20:17)! We have no giants, no conflicts, and no challenges in heaven! My beloved, this is your new lens to see your life on earth as it is in heaven! Remember you will be in the undefeated winning Royal Family when you carry My Son with you everywhere you go! All of our resources will be available to you when you receive My Son JESUS!

Our Perspective will determine how you see your new lifestyle! It is a heavenly and eternal perspective. We will teach you that your every problem becomes an opportunity to practice and demonstrate who you are in Christ, and how the power and guidance of the HOLY SPIRIT transforms you into a joyful giant killer! The larger the giant slain, the higher you rise in My HOLY SPIRIT! The bigger the giant, the harder he falls, and the higher you rise in My Kingdom! You will learn, grow and blossom into your true identity!

BERNICE speaking to GOD as FATHER

My friend Kary Oberbrunner told me that I could see my circumstances in one of *two* ways in this world:

First, as a *victim* from a B.E.D.: Blaming, Excusing, Denying. The world's way sees circumstances with fear-blame-shame-denial-anger-greed from the Victim's point of view, and this is why "religion" doesn't work.

Second, as a *victor* with an O.A.R.: Ownership, Accountability, Responsibility. The heavenly way sees circumstances from an eternal perspective with You as my Protector, and that only a relationship with You teaches me Your Ways!

GOD as FATHER speaking to BERNICE

My beloved, both ways of dealing with circumstances were seen when Moses led My people out of Egypt. They were ready to cross the Jordan River to the Promised Land. Twelve spies were sent to spy out the conditions in the land. (Numbers 13)

Ten spies used the world's way of reporting on the circumstances they saw. They had the Victim's view of their position that the land could not be taken. They saw themselves as grasshopper victims compared to a land full of victimizing giants. These spies saw themselves as hopeless and helpless: "not enough, never be enough, and don't have enough."

Two spies, Caleb and Joshua, used the heavenly way of reporting on the circumstances they saw. They had the Victor's view of their position that the land could be taken. They saw themselves as a Mighty Majority because their ever-present GOD was going with them. These spies saw themselves as helped and hopeful totally satisfactory, totally competent, and totally resourced champions.

I know you are like these two men. The same HOLY SPIRIT that breathed the breath of life into Caleb and Joshua was at work when I created you. Your story will be like theirs. You will remember that you have all of Heaven in the battle with you. You will see your life's circumstances through a new and heavenly lens!

That, My beloved child, is THE LANGUAGE OF HEAVEN. My beloved child, the depth of your pain is the height of the beauty of your calling

You were created to enjoy a full intimate relationship with Us! We want to be your First Love. We want you to enjoy a new life placed within The Godhead—We want to share Our life as One God with you! Study My Word—get to know how I created you, the *real you*!

Each morning when you open your eyes, greet Me with "Good morning FATHER GOD! Good morning JESUS! Good morning HOLY SPIRIT! This is the day You have made, and I will rejoice and be glad in it" (Psalm 118:24)!

I have given you another day! I will bless you today so that you can bless others. I then want you to open your arms wide, and speak like this: "I receive, I receive, I really receive Your High Favor and rich blessings for this day and night. FATHER, please create in me a clean heart, and renew a right spirit within me. Make me Your worthy ambassador today! Make me an empty vessel, ready for You to bless all the people I encounter today. Show me the people You have chosen for me to bless!" So, My beloved, before your feet hit the floor each morning, recognize I have blessed you with the ability to stand in a new day!

When My Son JESUS Christ is your Savior, He becomes the Foundation, the *Cornerstone* for all of your plans for the future! He is The One Who My HOLY SPIRIT spoke to the Psalmist about while writing Psalm 118:22-23 and spoke to Paul about while writing Ephesians 2:19-22. You stand on the Solid Rock of JESUS.

When you were born, you were given the name BERNICE which means "Bringer of Victory". In Revelation 2:17, My HOLY SPIRIT wrote through John these words: "To the one who is victorious, I will give some of the hidden manna. I will also give that person a white stone with a new name written on it,

19

known only to the one who receives it. I want you to stand on the white stone new name I give you on the Chief Cornerstone Who is JESUS, My Son!

Your enemy, satan, masquerades as an angel of light (2 Corinthians 11:12-14). He represents a *black counterfeit stone*—polished, beautiful, enticing stone, which is no foundation—nothing to stand on. He parades himself as light, power, and love, but it is false love, a false power. Yet, the world calls his false love and power real. It is nothing more, nothing less than manipulation and control—counterfeit love and power.

Sadly, some teach MY WORD praying and claiming to know Me, but they do not. This will not be you because now you know the difference. You will stand on the white stone of your name on the Chief Cornerstone Who is JESUS overflowing with pure, genuine Love that comes from Our Heart seated on Our Throne! Bring all relationships to Me. Hear My Voice! My HOLY SPIRIT will teach you how to relate heart to heart.

Like Caleb and Joshua, you will follow ME fully. I will also bring you into the Promised Land to take possession of it. My beloved child, you carry My always victorious HOLY SPIRIT. WE will be always be with you conquering in every battle, mightily winning every war!

Remember beloved, your current circumstances are created for you to co-labor with Me. We could rescue you, but you would learn nothing of being created in OUR IMAGE. Your circumstances are the rich soil ready for a breakthrough in My Son. We will teach you the Language of Heaven and empower you to lead your life on earth as We lead life in heaven.

The law of the spirit of life in Christ JESUS is about moving in the opposite direction of the spirit coming against you! My Son JESUS will teach you how to rise up against it and how to have a mindset of abundance rather than a poverty mindset.

All negativity was killed on the cross. However, I gave negativity a new purpose. This means daily focus your thinking on the opposite of every negative circumstance. Focus on *what I am doing for you* in each situation. Know My Word. Remember My Promises for each circumstance. Believe Me for provision to overcome each struggle. This is the Provision I make daily for you. This is the Promise I give to you. I will use every negative to grow you in My Spirit. You will learn how to step into the opposite of your negative. The opposite of your negative is Me. Stay close to Me and HOLY SPIRIT will teach you how to walk on earth as it is in heaven!

You have told me that in your wandering, you have done many bad things. Correct?

BERNICE speaking to GOD as FATHER

You have no idea how bad I have been. Sorry, I guess You do know. I have done many bad things and people have done many bad things to me. How can I ever be reconciled to You? How will I learn a better way?

GOD as FATHER speaking to BERNICE

Do you believe My Son JESUS loved you *so much* that He was crucified on the cross for *every one* of the bad things you have done? He would have done this, if you were the only person that ever did anything wrong. He loves you personally that much. Are you ready to ask JESUS, MY SON into your heart and really mean it? Are you ready to surrender everything in your life to HIM? Are you ready to make FATHER GOD, JESUS, and HOLY SPIRIT your first love above all else?

My beloved Bernice, *choose Life*! Invite My Son to come to you now. Ask My Son into your heart, into your being, into everything that is you, Bernice. *You were created to be one who brings victory and to be given a new white-stone name!*

BERNICE speaking to GOD as FATHER

Yes FATHER, I believe, and I give all my life to You. I humbly surrender. I receive!

GOD as FATHER speaking to BERNICE

Do you surrender your spirit for My HOLY SPIRIT? Do you surrender your soul: your thoughts for My Thoughts, your emotions for My Emotions, your will for My Will? Do you surrender your whole body to be a living holy sacrifice to Me?

BERNICE speaking to GOD as FATHER

I am humbled that You would take a wretch like me and wash me white as snow. I have no words to fully express my gratitude. I surrender all. I am so humbled that the Creator of the universe would love me so much after all I have done against You and others. Thank you that I am adopted into Your Royal Family. I want to know You completely. Fill me with Your Presence. Just this little taste of You gives me such hope and joy! Will you teach me? I want to know everything! Please be My Guide and lead me into the forever life I have always wanted!

GOD as FATHER speaking to BERNICE

My Beloved child, all of heaven is throwing a big party in your honor right now! You are now *a New Creation. The old you* died with My Son on the cross, and He acted as you. *Your old self* is dead. Yes, old habits still must go and will go by yielding to the Power of My HOLY SPIRIT and the Example of JESUS, My Son! We will support you as you navigate life with Us. We will teach you how to live out of the reality of who you have become now and are now in Christ. You died with Him, you were buried with Him, you rose with Him, and you are seated in Him on His Throne in heaven next to My Throne. Your *self in heaven* and your *self on earth* are coming together!

As you are willing, My HOLY SPIRIT will help that happen. Rest fully aware that you dwell in the Lord JESUS Christ, My Son! Our Love flows down like warm liquid gold from Our Throne into the full protection of the Presence of My Son that totally surrounds you. You now live, hidden in the center of My Son (Isaiah 46:8-11, John 14:20).

He will walk with you and talk with you! He will tell you that you are His own. He dances with you above each test, trial, trouble, and sickness. They don't belong to you anymore. They belong to Me.

Use your imagination again. In your spirit, see the back of My Son and see your back. Across each set of shoulders is a yoke. When a test, trial, trouble or sickness comes, just open your right hand, put that thing in it, then symbolically prayerfully place those burdens on the shoulders of My Son on His side of the yoke. *Your responsibility is to hold up your side of the yoke empowered by HOLY SPIRIT. Hold up your side by coming into My gates with thanksgiving and into My courts with praise.* (Ps.100:4 NIV) Rest in the Holy of Holies in the Secret Place of the Most High GOD. Honor and bless Me, worship and praise Me, and thank ME for your growing understanding of how I deal with each challenge you face. My Word will be a light unto your feet—it will light your way!

BERNICE speaking to GOD as FATHER

FATHER, life is different since I met JESUS. The old me would not have regret about how I treated You and other people. In my worldly ways, if I was sorry, I would say something like: "I'm sorry. Will You forgive me?" But I probably would not really mean it. It would be just to manipulate You and others to get something I wanted from You or them. But now, I've changed. Honestly, it confuses me. How do You do that? I really want to know. Now I am experiencing such deep sorrow. It hurts me so deeply that I treated You and others so selfishly and cruelly.

Since I met JESUS, I'm different. I can't really explain it, but I especially feel sorrow now that I understand all You have done for me. I didn't have to get cleaned up before You took me in. You accepted me just as I was. I was very wrong. You never gave up on me. You loved me even though I was a mess. I was so very wrong. You hunted me down until I was ready to see with the eyes of JESUS. I see I was rotten to the core. So I come to You heavenly FATHER admitting I was so wrong. I want to ask you: Will You forgive me? I know you do.

I owe Your HOLY SPIRIT so much. I heard You calling Me to humble myself and surrender. You have brought me to the place where I can sincerely say, "You are my First Love!" Now, I find I am Your Choice. You set me up in Your House, Your Kingdom, and then You made me Your Heir! My feet on Your Path. I am Radiant!

GOD as FATHER speaking to BERNICE

Beloved, I want you to rest in the Secret Place of the Most High, for you will find rest in the Shadow of the Almighty. I will shield you with My wings. I will shelter you with My feathers. My faithful promises will be your guide, and your protection. I will rescue you from every trap. You are no longer afraid of the terrors of the night. You do not fear the dangers of the day or dread the plague that stalks in darkness or the disaster that strikes at noonday. Though a thousand fall at your side, though ten thousand die all around you, this evil will not harm you. You will see with your eyes. You will see how the wicked are punished. But because you love Me, because you rest in the Secret Place of the Most High, *no* evil will conquer you. *No* plague will come near your dwelling. I will order My angels to protect you wherever you go. They will take you by both hands to keep you from striking your foot against a stone. Because I am in you, and you are in Me, You will trample the lion and poisonous snake. You will crush the fierce lion and snake under your foot. Because you love Me, I will rescue you. Because you trust Me, I will protect you. When you call upon Me, I will answer. I will be with you in time of trouble. I will rescue you and honor you. I will satisfy you with a long life, and I will give you My Salvation! (Psalm 91)

BERNICE speaking to GOD as FATHER

FATHER, I am undone by Your Goodness and Kindness. I am so hungry and thirsty to know You personally, *really* know You! I want to be a Child that brings You only pleasure! I want to know who You created me to be, the *real* me! I want to know all about JESUS. I want to trust You the way JESUS trusts You. I was called the curse of the family by my Father, but You told me that is not my real identity. *I long to know who I am in The Lord JESUS Christ!*

Part Two

IDENTITY

I WILL GIVE HIM A WHITE STONE,
WITH A NEW NAME WRITTEN ON
THE STONE
THAT NO ONE KNOWS EXCEPT THE
ONE WHO RECEIVES IT
Revelation 2:17

BERNICE speaking to GOD as FATHER

Hello *precious Abba FATHER*, I read something on Facebook today that blew me away. And now, this is what I truly passionately want to do:

1. Put on my new nature in CHRIST so that it will become part of everything I do,
2. Learn to know my CREATOR, moment by moment,
3. Become more like YOU.

There it was—a scripture that said—*this is exactly what You want for me*: Anyway, what Wendy Taylor put on her Facebook post has blessed me every day since. "Put on your new nature, and *be renewed* as you learn to know your Creator and *become like Him*" (Colossians 3:10 NLT). What *blessed words* have come to me today!

You led my friend Wendy to post it on Facebook to let me know *I am on the right track with You*. Her walk with You has been such a wonderful example for me. She has taught me so much about the different ways to have a relationship with You, GOD—as FATHER, as Lord JESUS Christ, and as HOLY SPIRIT. *You have used her to lead me to a hunger, a thirst for Your Word, and a desire to know who I am in You*. Her ministry to free women from the sex-trafficking trade in India has taught me how I am to listen to, be guided by, and used by You to restore others from darkness to Your light.

Thank You for putting Wendy in my life to *teach* me. I have worked to become more like her in my walk with You. I learned from her to read the Gospels over and over again. *I have done that and have asked HOLY SPIRIT to teach me how JESUS walked on earth, and to guide me to become like Him.*

FATHER, as I read about JESUS, I see how *He treasured His conversations with You*—how *He left the presence of His friends* early in the morning *to be alone in Your Presence* just to hear Your Voice and speak with You. Only after time with You did He interact with HIS disciples and other people. *I am intentionally copying His Pattern into my life as well.*

There are also *three things* that I see in JESUS' nature, that I want to be in mine.

The first is *Humility.* It is interesting how the HOLY SPIRIT taught me the importance of being humble. One morning, I was reading the Bible. With spiritual eyes, I saw a picture of two rows of chairs placed on what looked like choir risers. A great peace came over me. It sounds strange—I sensed You were using my mind to think YOUR thoughts.

It did not scare me. Your HOLY SPIRIT had already taught me that *the second nature of JESUS when He was on earth was to surrender to You moment by moment.* I am practicing this now. It is easier said than done. I am asking the HOLY SPIRIT to teach me to surrender to You *while I am speaking* with someone here on earth. As I speak, I want to be aware of You in heaven on Your Throne. *I only want to do what You are doing and to say what You are saying.*

That morning when I saw the chairs in my spirit, I heard you say: "*Bernice, hear Me. I want you to go low—back row, last seat. Be aware. Watch Me work. I have you in the palm of My Hand.*" I had already, by faith and the Blood of Jesus, shut down satan, his fallen angels, and his plan for my day and night. So FATHER, I knew it was Your Voice speaking to me. I had surrendered my spirit to the HOLY SPIRIT. I had surrendered my soul—my mind for Your Thoughts, my emotions for Your Emotions, my will for Your Will. My whole being is Yours!!!

After my surrender, I felt *a new kind of reality—I was wearing the Spirit of Jesus like clothes* . . . a beautiful suit of Him. By His grace, I felt I had put on garments of His Presence to wear, to live in, to make Him real on earth. I realized that hearing Your Voice, being intimate with You, is for us "little people", and not just for "spiritual giants". You told me in Your Word that I may be like pottery, but *You are the Treasure living within me* revealing to everyone around me that *You are the extraordinary power of my life, not me* (2 Corinthians 4:7). I am amazed!

I felt no fear because I felt I had met the Author, the Creator of my soul. I knew You were sharing what You wanted me to do. I knew it was not satan. That morning when You called me by name, I knew *You were thinking thoughts through me.* Because You have drawn me to *invest* time in my relationship with You, *I have now learned the sound of Your Voice.* So often, I hear Your Voice when I am reading Your Word. You *reveal truth* to me I have never known before. FATHER, You have *revealed pride* in my heart for some seven years now. I know You were teaching me how to recognize humility in JESUS, and then how to *recognize and act in humility myself* because I am made in Your Image. JESUS is more humble than any man I have ever known.

I read in Your Word that *JESUS surrendered to You* when He walked on earth. *This is why I surrender my days and nights to You daily.* I hope You don't think my way of coming to You at the beginning and ending of the day is silly. If I am wrong in how I do anything, please teach me to do everything as You desire. I am so grateful that You (as the Godhead) are so *real* to me. I feel so blessed that Charlie and I read Your Word together and pray before we turn out the lights each night.

After we turn out the lights, I love my private time with You. I think it is *my favorite time* with You. I get to experience and rest in Your Love. Silly as this part may sound, *You have given me a wonderful imagination* so I use it. By faith, I imagine that my pillow is JESUS' chest. I lie in His Arms in a pool of His Love. With pleasure, I think back through the day about all the conversations and interactions I've had with those You have brought into my life. I call each of them by name, and ask You to bless them in every way . . . physically, mentally, emotionally, and most importantly spiritually. I ask, in Your Mercy, that You show them High Favor and Rich Blessing.

As I quietly lie in Your Presence, and surrender my night to you . . . I feel Your Robe of Peace tucked in over, around and under me. *My heart burns with the Presence of Your Son resting in my heart.* I am so grateful that He has taken away the imprisoning walls from around my heart as well as the stones of anger, hurt, and unforgiveness I had placed there. I have placed each of these at the foot of His cross. His Blood is covering them. I am so very grateful that He removes them from me and sends them as far as the east is from the west (Psalm 103:12).

By faith, I simply hold the width, length, height, and depth of Your Love—FATHER GOD, JESUS, and

HOLY SPIRIT—in my heart. By faith, *I love* You back *with Your Love*. I love myself with Your Love, I love Charlie, my children, their spouses, my grandchildren and all those I encounter with Your Love. I love the peace I feel when I surrender my night to You as I ask You to create in me a clean heart and to renew a right spirit within me. If I wake up in heaven, I will come to You with a clean heart.

FATHER, I am so grateful You always hear me when I say, "If I open my eyes on earth tomorrow, I will know *You have a plan for me to bless those You bring into my life* that day. I start each day with a renewed excitement and expectancy for what my day may bring.

BERNICE speaking to GOD as JESUS

Please *JESUS, give me Your eyes to see others as You see them*. Please help me to get out of the way. JESUS, I want to *represent* You well in every encounter I have with each person You bring before me. Please use my eyes as open portals to carry Your Love from Your Throne in heaven, through my heart, and straight into the heart of the person as I speak. Let us connect heart to heart. May Your Eternal Love touch their heart and cause a shift inside them. May each of them be transformed by Your Love, never to be the same again. Words cannot express how I go to sleep each night. My peace is unexplainable. I know You hear my prayer as I continue to open my eyes each morning with expectancy.

Lord, please correct me if You want me to change how I greet You each morning. You are so real to me. You never leave me. *My life has changed so much. I*

PART TWO

received You as My Lord and Savior—the Most Precious Gift I have ever been given! And You adopted me into Your Family. *I just can't get enough of You.* So, I greet You as my Best Friend.

When my eyes open each morning, do You think I am silly to *believe* that You are *literally* with me in my bedroom? Our morning times together center me with renewed hope. I love that Charlie gets up before me, and closes the bedroom door. *That means* when I open my eyes, even before my feet touch the floor, *You __are__ there.* I look to the right corner of the ceiling across from my bed. Aloud I say, "Good morning FATHER". I then look at the middle of the ceiling across from my bed and say, "Good morning JESUS". And finally looking to the left corner of the ceiling, I say "Good morning HOLY SPIRIT". "This is the day the Lord has made. I will rejoice, and be glad in it" (Psalm 118:24). I love this part too—You taught this only two weeks ago. After declaring Your creation of the day, Your HOLY SPIRIT directed me to stretch my arms wide open and *receive.*

JESUS, You have shown me a picture in heaven where You are seated at Your Dining Room Table. I am seated to Your right. We are in Your beautiful stone mansion. I gratefully receive the exact portion of nourishment from You at Your Table. I love how You feed me my daily bread. In Your Word, You tell me to come to You as a child—that is the internal image I keep in my heart each morning. I am practicing seeing myself as a little girl. Yet, I sit as an adult at Your Table.

You feed me the exact nourishment I need to fulfill my purpose on earth for that day. Even as I write this, tears come to my eyes that You would love me in this

33

intimate way. So I am really beginning to understand that *all those sad names* others called me *are the exact opposite of who YOU call me and created me to be.* Your Grace is *amazing*! You loved me before I came to be— this is truly unmerited favor!

I will never forget the morning, while I was reading my Bible, when suddenly for the first time You allowed me to see You sitting at the head of a very long table in Your beautiful dining room in heaven. The dining room was in a beautiful mansion, and I was seated right next to You. Everything was vibrant with color. On this table was luscious food. Each morsel of food was different, separated from the other, and each smaller than a tart. Each sat in fancy paper that came up the sides of the food like cupcakes, but I could see the top of each. They were stunningly beautiful and extended from one end of the table to the other. Although I had not tasted them, somehow I knew that each bite would taste better than anything I had ever eaten.

As we sat there not eating, You said to me, "I want you to come to Me each morning. I will give you the exact nourishment you will need to fulfill your purpose for that day. This is why you were born, and why you have had to overcome *each and every challenge* you have faced. These challenges were part of satan's plan, but *I have used them to free your soul to soar.*

As foolish as it seems, I didn't "get it". I did not have the discernment until two weeks ago about Your directions. Until then, I just marveled that You, as GOD of the universe, would make it so plain to me that You give to me my daily bread to carry out Your purpose for my life. I was so aware of Your amazing kindness to me, and that You trusted me enough to show me Your generosity so personally.

It was about two years ago that You revealed that scene in heaven to me. Forgive me, Lord. I guess I am slow—it was only two weeks ago that Your HOLY SPIRIT taught me to *open my arms wide and receive* each morning. So now, each morning I see by faith what I only saw in part, the picture of that very dining room where I am seated with You JESUS at Your Table in heaven where You feed me my portion for the day. It is so easy to thank You now for giving me my daily bread each morning. After I declare that I receive Your High Favor and Rich Blessing in order to bless and nourish others that day, I am ready to put my feet on the floor.

My best days are days I call "Preventative Care Days". On those days when I start my day with You in this way, I walk in peace no matter the circumstance. *I rise above.*

Wow JESUS, I so much want to know Your Nature, and imitate You! I want to be Your ambassador on earth and to bring Your Kingdom and Will to earth as it is in heaven! FATHER, I want that right now! Yet, I am learning that through hard days and better days, building Your Kingdom and doing Your Will is a process. I so want my life to reflect all of You!

I know that *my life is to be lived with humility, surrender, giving and receiving.*

I know that I still have old habits that are not of You, but I am excited to have found a way moment by moment and day by day to deal with them. When I really feel regret and sorrow for a failure or sin, quickly

I imagine a picture of a courtroom in heaven. But in my imagination before I go there, I come to Your Throne Room of Mercy and Grace in Heaven. I celebrate You; I worship You; I praise You; I honor You; I bless You; I thank You for Your Kindness, Your Goodness, Your Justice, and Your Peace.

BERNICE speaking to GOD as FATHER

After this time in Your Presence FATHER GOD, in my spirit I see a picture of You in the Court Room of Justice in heaven. You are seated in the judge's seat. I see JESUS leaning on the Judge's bench. He is interceding for me and for others, twenty-four seven. I see satan at the prosecution desk condemning us twenty four seven.

By faith, I come into Your Court Room of Justice, and I bow before You. I am learning the power of JESUS' Blood, Name and Resurrection Power. By faith, I shut down satan, his fallen angels, and his plan for me that day and night by those three things. I take responsibility, renounce, repent, and admit that I am wrong for whatever I have done against You or others. I ask You to forgive me, and I believe You do. I believe and live out Your Truth that there is no condemnation for those who are in JESUS Christ (Romans 8:1). I remember Your lesson of my opened left hand representing that weakness or sin. You said to remember that You are always there at my point of pain. The HOLY SPIRIT keeps reminding me that I am made in Your Image.

I put my opened right hand close to my left hand knowing You are right there next to my pain. FATHER,

I am so grateful that I can place every negative, test, trial, trouble, and sickness on JESUS' shoulders on His side of the yoke.

I stand on my side of the yoke, coming into Your Gates with thanksgiving and into Your Courts with praise. I am humbled that I have the privilege to rest in You in the Holy Of Holies, in the Secret Place of The Most High. When I think of the darkness from which I've come, I am stunned. I no longer get discouraged. I am humbled when I remember how in my dark days I had nowhere to turn.

GOD as FATHER speaking to BERNICE

Beloved, *I love that you come to Me with a thankful heart*! You even tell me you are writing a book about My wonders in your life. I love to watch you whistling, laughing, and jumping for joy. Your song to Me thrills My heart. You speak to Me every day about your gratitude that I took over and set everything right. When you need Me, I love to be there and take charge.

Beloved, you learn fast, and *I am grateful that you already know that I am a safe-house for the battered, a sanctuary during bad times*. You are never sorry you knocked. I remember the other day you said that you love My Kindness, for you had been kicked around long enough. You told Me you love Me because I pulled you back from the gates of death.

I smiled when you told Me that you will write a book on Hallelujahs on the corner of Main and First. You even said you would hold a street meeting. You said you would be the song leader, and lead the salvation songs (Psalm 9:1–2, 4, 7–10, 13–14). Beloved, you bring Me so much joy! You are *the apple of My Eye*! (Psalm 17:8).

BERNICE speaking to GOD as FATHER

FATHER, my old insecure attachments, restricting strongholds, and unhealthy foundations are being destroyed. Yet, I don't always know what to do when the people I used to hang around with start shooting arrows from the shadows. I am reminded of the heart-breaking names I have been called, and how I even began to think and foolishly act out those names in my relationships and circumstances.

There were so many demoralizing names. I remember many: dirty, liar, cursed, plain, unappreciated, calloused, self-injurer, simple, tramp, whore, bankrupt, deceptive, troubled, clumsy, cutter, slut, used, tainted, loser, disposable, stupid, invisible, suicidal, broken, unbalanced, single, unlovable, ugly, damned, awkward, impatient, unloved, impure, unproductive, friendless, hopeless, helpless, anxious, unworthy. Some of them may not sound bad to those who said them—but they all cut deeply. FATHER, my heart begins to sink as I even start thinking about them.

GOD as FATHER speaking to BERNICE

Beloved, that is not who you are now or who you ever were—you are My child! I AM Creator of the Universe. Yes, because you were so abused when you were young, you have lies and limiting beliefs hidden in your mind. I am so pleased with you because daily you study My Word. I know that I AM *that* important to you. The HOLY SPIRIT reveals *My Truth* to you which is *the opposite* of the lies you believed. You will discern and learn The Truth of The Life I have for you. Use The Truth against those lies.

From birth until you were six, you had *no* reasoning ability. When you were told there was a Santa Claus who would leave you presents on Christmas morning, you believed it. You were so excited anticipating Santa Claus that, when you heard a noise outside, you hid under the covers. You believed it totally. So on Christmas Eve, you could hardly fall asleep. Heart pounding and palms sweating, you just knew the noise on your roof was Santa and his reindeer.

When you woke up on Christmas morning, you found presents under the Christmas tree. False as it was, the presence of presents reinforced the belief that indeed there was a Santa Claus. You had no ability to figure out that a fat jolly man could not in one night deliver presents to each child in the world. You just believed. You totally believed it.

Beloved, now do you see—*because I AM real*, this is how I want you to come to Me—*with good reason and full of hope*? Come as a child greets Christmas morning. Come to Me each morning with as much joy, excitement, delight, heart-pounding, curiosity, imagination, expectancy, and belief—so much that you can *see Our Love—taste* it, and *touch* it! *Come with anticipation—just like Christmas morning!*

Bernice, you have dedicated to Me *your total being!* You hold nothing back. By doing this, *I am free to make a living display of you.* Because you *totally surrender*, I will send My Spirit *streaming* through you. Because you practice focusing on Me moment by moment day and night, you have *become* a bubbling spring of joy! People now love you. They want to experience My Presence through you. You are My *Treasure*, and they are drawn to Me because *they see the life of freedom you enjoy*. Hold that image. Hold that picture of *your desires deeply hidden in your heart*. My gifts to you are always good. "Which of you, if your son asks for bread, will give him a stone? Or if he asks for a fish, will give him a snake? If you, then, though you are evil, know how to give good gifts to your children, how much more will your FATHER in heaven give good gifts to those who ask?" (Matthew 7:7-11) *I want you to ask.*

When you were seven years old, you were on the playground at school, a little girl told you there is no Santa Claus. She said, "Your Mom and Dad buy the presents, and they put them under the Christmas tree". You got really mad at her because you believed there is a Santa. That Christmas season, you saw a certain box in the car, and then it vanished. On Christmas morning, you found a package wrapped under the tree that was the same size and shape as the box that vanished from the car. You remember what your friend said about there not being a Santa; that it is your parents giving you the presents. You begin to reason: "Maybe, my friend was right. Maybe, there is no Santa. Maybe it's my parents. You continued to reason, talked to older children, until finally you understood—indeed, there is no Santa Claus.

The same is true for how you *learned* your *identity*. Who are you? The sad names you were called, the way you were treated by ignorant parents, teachers, play-mates, and others, the way you were abused, the way you were treated from birth until six *became truth* for you. You *thought* that *was* your *Identity*. You thought

40

that was *who you are*. You began to *act out* those false names because *you believed the lies and the limiting beliefs* as your truth. It was a false identity *concocted* by your enemy satan.

The people that treated you that way did not know My Ways. They did not know My Truth. They lived in darkness. They knew nothing of My Nature. My Son is in you. You are in the center of My Son. He is all around you. You are a member of Our Royal Family. We will show you *how to deal with* those sad names and limiting beliefs.

Just choose one sad name—any sad name you have *acted out* as an adult. I will show you how *HOLY SPIRIT helps you find, know, and experience My Truth.* Stay close. He will free you from the old you and acquaint you with your *new Identity*. A part of your soul will be *healed,* and you will be able to *access* more of My Presence. Beloved, what name has hurt you deeply?

BERNICE speaking to GOD as FATHER

Let's do "Stupid".

GOD as FATHER speaking to BERNICE

Great! You can ask the HOLY SPIRIT to tell you My Truth. To Me, you are the Opposite of every sad name you were ever called.

BERNICE speaking to GOD as HOLY SPIRIT

HOLY SPIRIT, will You give me a picture, a memory of the first time I ever felt *stupid?*

This is incredible! Wow! Seriously, I'm already beginning to see a picture of when I was three years old. My whole family—the three other children, Dad, Mom and I were in the living room of our home. In 1937 during the big national depression, a nickel or a dime would buy almost a whole meal.

My Dad held a nickel and dime in his hand. He said, "I am going to give Betty and Bernice this nickel and dime. And since Bernice is the youngest she gets to choose first." This was a big deal. I was excited, but that soon changed. My sister was six, but being a smart little three year old, I chose the nickel. It is bigger, right?

The room burst out in jeering *laughter*. I was *stunned*. Excitement changed to *fear*. With my heart *pounding*, I asked, "What did I do *wrong*?" I *didn't know* what I had done wrong, but my little heart raced with fear. *Everyone, but me, knew* what I had done wrong. My Dad took the coins back saying "That's not fair, let's give Bernice another chance". I chose the nickel over and over, because I *could not reason* a dime was more valuable.

Each time I chose the nickel, the jeers got louder and louder. Every time they laughed, I wanted to run or go through the floor, but I was *too afraid*. This went on for some time with no one showing me the error of my choice. No one ever tried to teach me the value of a dime. I was *not* a part of the family. I was alone. I was their *entertainment*. *There*, at the tender age of three, *enters stupid* in my life. The results were extensive and unstoppable. In school and other places as an adult, I thought I was stupid. It *felt* like

I *always was.* Even though I worked very hard, my grades were average. I have spent much of my life wearing *the mask of an intellectual.* Only now, since I found JESUS, am I *living without my masks. I am able to be me!*

GOD as HOLY SPIRIT speaking to BERNICE

Beloved, ask Me *what lies you believed about yourself* when that happened.

BERNICE speaking to GOD as HOLY SPIRIT

HOLY SPIRIT, what lies did I believe about myself when my family used me for their entertainment?

GOD as HOLY SPIRIT speaking to BERNICE

Bernice, these are the lies that you believed about yourself which you thought were simply thoughts in your head.

BERNICE speaking to GOD as HOLY SPIRIT

1. I'm not as smart as everyone else. I am stupid. 2. I am different. 3. I don't belong.

GOD as HOLY SPIRIT speaking to GOD as FATHER

FATHER, tell Bernice Our Truth about who she really was at that moment.

GOD as FATHER speaking to BERNICE

First, Beloved, My Truth is *you are <u>brilliant!</u>* You knew the nickel was *the biggest*, even though you were *just three* years old. They did not stop to affirm the *smartness* of your choice, and then teach you the *value* of the dime. You felt alone, but *I was there*.

Second, I was *always* with you in *every* painful situation. I *allowed* insensitive, self-centered people to *revile My Son*. Then, *I was with Him on the cross* when *He bought your salvation. Now, you belong to Me.* So *it is also with you* that *your pain becomes* your *power,* and your pain *becomes* your *passion* to influence the life of others for their highest good. HOLY SPIRIT is *using the depth of your pain to raise you to the height of the beauty of your calling.* In potentially your *worst* pain, you find My Presence *sufficient* to protect you and satisfy you with long life (Psalm 91).

I give you an opportunity to grow in the Image of Me. Every time the bad happens, you get to *practice* turning your eyes *on Me*, and *not on the problem*. We actually use your problems (if you remember that I AM always at the very depth of your pain) to *reveal* to you a quality of My Nature in you that you would not know if this bad thing had not happened.

You see, <u>*My beloved Child,*</u> "If you are *aware* of Me, I make even the "bad" *good.* You are My child so it's *all good.* This way, *you* have a *choice: use* My wisdom, understanding, counsel, power, and knowledge, or fearfully *repeat* your tour around the mountain to relive the "bad" again. You never *fail* the test. You can always take it over *as many times as you choose <u>not</u> to* see yourself *in Me*. Your other choice is to *surrender* it to Me in thanksgiving and praise as *you and I partner in the yoke, working it out together.*

Third, Bernice, you are <u>*My Chosen One.*</u> I put you into that home to be My example in that home and all over the world of how *I can change you from darkness to light.* You are *My most brilliant, shining star.* I see you as a mountain of diamonds. Your life in Me is going to produce a range of mountains. Each mountain in that range will turn into a mountain of diamonds. That is your *reward*. Beloved, I have searched you and know you. I know when you sit down and when you rise up. I understand your thoughts from afar. I know your path and your lying down. I am acquainted with all your ways. There is not a word on your tongue that I did not know already. I hedge you in, behind and before. I have laid My Hand upon you (Psalm 139).

BERNICE speaking to GOD as FATHER

O FATHER, I am *so* grateful that this is *true*. Where can I go from Your Spirit? Where can I flee from Your Presence? FATHER GOD, I *am* so grateful for Your *Truth*. "If I ascend into heaven, You are there. If I make my bed in hell, behold You are there. If I take the wings of the morning, and dwell in the uttermost parts of the sea, even there Your Hand shall lead me, and Your Right Hand shall hold me. If I say, "Surely the darkness shall fall on me, even the night shall be light about me. Indeed the darkness shall not hide you from Me. But the night shines as the day" (Psalm 139).

GOD as FATHER speaking to BERNICE

Beloved, We love that you hunger and thirst for Us to be your First Love! We love your curiosity about who We are, and who you are in Us! We love that you come to Us asking the right questions (I told you your mind is sharp; you are brilliant)! We love that you are desiring the right things! This morning, when you came to My Son's mansion in heaven to get your daily bread, I saw how brilliant you are! You got Our Message! You quickly understood that *it is not just about you*. You put no conditions on your life. My Son will take you with Him not only for a day, but for eternity (My Utmost For His Highest, June 12).

BERNICE speaking to GOD as FATHER

FATHER, before I only wanted to know JESUS *so that I would be blessed*. I wanted to *do* something for Him. I wanted to *see* myself and others to *see* me as a *good person*. I was wrong. I realize I was *doing* all the right things (reading my Bible, praying, being kind). I actually was *doing* right things for wrong reasons. I was just imitating a "false christ" standing on the "imitation black stone" of my deceptive enemy, rather than standing on the white Cornerstone of the true Christ.

As I visit the mansion of JESUS each morning in heaven, He has expanded our time together. Often, He takes me onto the portico of a beautifully built mansion made from golden-colored stone, three stories high, and overlooking majestically manicured rolling hills with ancient trees dotting the landscape. I always see JESUS' back and my back walking the lengthy portico.

My goal now is JESUS Himself, not His joy, peace or blessing—just my GOD and Friend. I need nothing but Him! (My Utmost For His Highest, July 12).

Your Ways are a mystery to me. They are higher than my ways—I love them. I don't "get it". But I do know this—it's not about me, it's about You! Even as I seek to make JESUS my main thing, I find myself being more highly favored and enjoying more rich blessings. It is as though every year gets better than the last, even while some challenging things continue to happen in my life. It is as though You are reading my mind and blessing me with the desires of my heart. Your Kingdom is puzzling. I must die to live, give to receive, forgive to be forgiven, be last to become first. 'Just sayin'—I love Your Economy!'

FATHER, one thing often comes to my mind: Was there a reason I had such a rough beginning? I have been called awful names, and to my shame I lived up to them. My earthly Father called me *the curse of the family*. You know the awful names I have been called.

I was reading in the book of The Revelation today. It said "I will give him a white stone and on the stone a New Name is written which no one knows except him who receives it" (Revelation 2:17). I know that recently You told me how important it is to learn how to *receive* from You. Will You tell me the name You have written on *my white stone*?

GOD as FATHER speaking to BERNICE (BLESSING)

You are right to ask Me this question because *the name* written on your white stone *is My Intent and*

47

Purpose for you. It was written on *the very first day* your earthly father called you *the curse of the family* for the first time. On that day, *I was right there when your heart was breaking.* Remember I told you when bad things happen they cannot happen without Me being right there? I AM the *Opposite* of that bad thing.

My plan is to give you a reward multiplied more than seven times for what the enemy stole from you that day (Proverbs 6:31). That first day your father called you a *curse*, I wrote *The Name I call you* on your white stone. I call you *BLESSING.*

That day *I claimed you* as *My favorite daughter.* I waited for you to return home. *I love blessing you in order that you can bless others.* In This Family we don't take, we give. The *enemy*, through your Dad, called you a *curse.* That day I declared *you are BLESSING in order to bless—that is your reward, your purpose, your destiny, your future.* I am excited as We co-create Your Future.

Here is another way of putting it: "You're here to be Light, bringing out the GOD-colors in the world. I AM not a secret to be kept. We're going public with this, as public as a city on a hill . . . You don't think I'm going to hide you under a bucket, do you? I'm putting you on a light stand—Shine! Keep open house; be generous with your life. By opening up to others, you'll prompt people to open up with Me. I am a generous FATHER in heaven" (Matthew 5:16).

All of Us in heaven are dancing over you living out your purpose—*BLESSING! You are BLESSING, in order to bless!*

Part Three

INTENT

AS IRON SHARPENS IRON,
SO ONE MAN SHARPENS ANOTHER
Proverbs 27:17

BLESSING speaking to GOD as FATHER

FATHER, it was never Your *Intent and Purpose* for us to live broken lives. For so long, my intent and purpose was all about me, and I never made the connection between my suffering and what You could and would do to make the lives of others better through me.

It was *when I placed all the pieces before You that You began to make my life complete* and my life began to make real sense for the first time ever. When I realized *only You could put my broken pieces together again*, You gave me a fresh start. Now, I am alert to Your Ways. I don't take You for granted. Every day, I review the ways You work. I do not want to miss a thing. I am so grateful that I feel put back together, and I am watching my steps. FATHER, You rewrote the text of my life when I made the choice to open the book of my heart to Your Eyes (Psalm 18:20–24).

FATHER, it is such a *relief* to me that You are in charge. It would be much easier to die for You than to lay down my life for others. Your HOLY SPIRIT is showing me how You want me to live by Your Example. I look in the Gospels and I see that You looked beyond the actions of each person without judging them. JESUS said about His enemies: "Father, forgive them for they know not what they do" (Luke 23:34). I am so thankful that JESUS lives in me, and I live in Him. One of my favorite parts of each day is my private moments with You in the morning and after I turn my light off at night.

I love to begin my day worshipping You, praising You, honoring You, and blessing You! I love to surrender my spirit for Your HOLY SPIRIT! I love to surrender my thoughts for Your Thoughts, my emotions for Your Emotions, my will for Your Will, and my body completely to you!

BLESSING speaking to GOD as JESUS

JESUS, each morning by faith, I place my troubles, tests, trials, and sicknesses onto Your shoulders on Your side of our yoke. I love that *my job is to hold up my side of the yoke empowered by You*, worshiping You, praising You, honoring You, blessing You, and thanking You for how You have taken my burdens and made them light. Thank You for how You give me wisdom, understanding, counsel, might, knowledge, and holy fear of You for each and every trial (Isaiah 11:2). I thank You I am able to wear Your Truth as strength for legs, Your Righteousness as a breastplate over my heart, Your Gospel of Your Peace to cover my feet; I am able to receive Your Faith as my shield, Your Salvation as helmet for my head, and Your Word as my sword. (Ephesians 6:10-20). I thank You that Your Armor protects me from satan and every enemy seeking to hinder, sabotage, or destroy Your plan for my day and night.

I thank You for living in me, using my ears to *hear together* what FATHER is saying, using my eyes to *see together* what He is revealing, using my mouth to *speak together* what He is saying, using my body to *do together* what He is doing, and even using my silence to *listen together* to hear the *heart* of the one speaking without impulsive response. While I am speaking to someone, You use my eyes to send FATHER'S Pure, Eternal Love from His Throne in heaven through my

51

heart and through my eyes into their eyes and into their heart. Your Pure Love shifts something in them, conveys something to them, and they are transformed and never to be the same again. *Your Pure Love changes each of us.*

Thank You that my arms and Your Arms are one so that, when I hug someone on earth, they receive a Holy hug on earth as it is in heaven. They get to experience Your Pure Love from heaven— You are hugging them using my arms. When I hug them, my mouth is near to one ear. Sometimes You whisper to me "You can say what is happening now" and I tell them "This morning, I surrendered my arms to JESUS and I asked Him to let each person I hug experience His heavenly love through my arms. Occasionally, JESUS whispers to me that I can tell that person my prayer and after I do, I say, "I am using my arms knowing JESUS is hugging you. Just know, I will hold you until you pull away". JESUS, their bodies become totally relaxed every time and they don't want me to stop hugging them.

Each encounter with You produces positive responses. Everyone seems stunned, in awe of You. They thank me, and say "I have never felt love like that before". One lady told me that this was the first time in her life that she had felt loved. To her, I said, "Do you realize that JESUS kept you for Himself! He wanted to be the First One from whom you felt love because your purpose is to carry His Pure, Eternal Love. You will teach His Pure Love to others who have never experienced love. JESUS also wants you to know that each time you were hurt, He was right there. His Heart was breaking for you, but He knew one day you would come home. *The depth of your pain is the beauty of your calling!"*

JESUS, *that* is what *You* told *me*! You are so good to me, and I am so grateful You guide me to rescue the perishing from darkness to Your Glorious Light!

This is how she described the experience to me, "As you held me, a peace and warmth came over me. I felt that GOD had sent His Love down from heaven through your arms. I actually felt something shift in me. I feel transformed, and I will never be the same again". No others I have hugged have told me such a dramatic story, but all have been peaceful and grateful.

Thank You that my feet are Your Feet on earth, and You direct my path (Proverbs 3:5-6). Use my hands to heal whomever You choose to heal when I pray. *You and I are like a perfectly fitting hand in glove*—I am the glove over your presence in me.

Each moment that I speak with someone, please make me aware that *You and I are one.* May Your Words be my words. Make me conscious of the truth that the Holy, Eternal, True Love of FATHER GOD, JESUS and HOLY SPIRIT is flowing from Your Throne, through my heart, and out of my eyes into the heart of the one to whom I speak. *JESUS, let me love each one as You love them.* I want people to hear You say through me: "I see you. I see your soul. You are important to Me".

BLESSING speaking to GOD as FATHER

This is how I've come to understand and experience Love: FATHER, *You sacrificed Your Own Life for me in and through Your Son.* This is why I ought to live sacrificially for others, not just for myself. If I see some brother or sister in need and have the means to do something about it, but turn a cold shoulder and do nothing, Your Love does not appear and I am responsible (1 John 3:16). This is beyond challenging at times for me even though in Your Son *You are my Precious Example.*

FATHER, I want to tell You how I feel about something that happened last Friday morning. You know my friend Rudy Diaz in San Diego is a mighty man in You. From Columbus, Ohio every Friday morning, I join him by phone to be under his Bible teaching based on Oswald Chamber's book *My Utmost For His Highest.* He places his phone on his table and I listen in sensing the high privilege You have given me to be a part of this group. This Friday, the lesson was "Laying Down Your Life". He explained that, in every moment and in every transaction, we always have a choice to (1) "lay down our life" or (2) respond as we did before JESUS came into our life.

Rudy is a brilliant man of Mexican descent working as head of the estimating department of a multimillion-dollar construction company. Using himself as an example, he gave the following insight: "If you are of Mexican heritage living in this country, when people see you they immediately think 'He can't speak English and probably just came across the border.'" These were Rudy's words, not mine.

A young man Rudy had mentored came to him with intention to bless Rudy for how he had led him spiritually. However, the young man began his comment like this: "Rudy, when I first met you, I didn't even know whether or not you spoke English. But wow man, because of you as my spiritual coach, my life is back on track. God has turned my life around because of how you taught me His Word, how you invested your time in me, and how you loved, and encouraged me."

Rudy said, at that moment, "*I had to make a choice: (1) respond the way I might have before I met JESUS Christ or (2) respond out of the new creation I am in JESUS Christ.* That was my choice: lay down my emotions for JESUS Christ's emotions or respond from the emotions of the Old Rudy. In my humanity as the Old Rudy, I could have said to him: Well, when I first saw you, I didn't know if you were a crack-head, an alcoholic, or a pervert spending all your time looking at pornography.

Rudy continued, "Honestly, it hurt at first when he spoke those words to me. I imagined what he was really saying to me was: 'I don't know if you are smart enough to speak English.' But in that moment, I chose to speak back to him from the *real* Rudy, *the new creation I am in JESUS Christ, Who lives in me!*"

I responded to Rudy, "Thank you! That means a lot to me." It did because Rudy has become a good role model for me. Throughout the day, I practice what has now become what I know as "going through the narrow gate" (Matthew 7:7-14). It was not easy at first, but I now experience such peace and joy like never before. I continue to ask, seek, and knock more than ever. *My deepest passion is to know JESUS and to be more like Him.* Your HOLY SPIRIT continues to show me Your Nature. He teaches me I am to learn through every negative situation I face. *This truly is a glorious life I live!* Rudy's example is a rare model for me of what it means for me to *lay down my life, moment by moment, one conversation, one circumstance, one decision, one choice at a time.*

GOD as JESUS speaking to BLESSING

Blessing, you are a good student of My Ways. You are practicing how I taught My disciples to pray, "Thy will be done on earth as it is in heaven". Because you humbly surrender your days and nights to me, I am able to patiently guide your '*soulish spirit*' in tribulation, need, and distress as you are tested in each of these areas. Pay attention to what I accomplished on the cross for you. Yes, I died to give you salvation. That is huge, yet it is just the beginning. I also gave you a new mindset; I made you a new creation. Because I live in you, *all of who I AM is available to you.* All of your old negatives, old behaviors, and old identities died on My Cross with Me. When you invited Me into your heart, into *you Blessing, all of Who I AM is your New Identity.* Pay attention to your heart. My Presence abides in your heart; I abide in all you are! *All of MY resources are now yours. My Intent and Purpose for you ultimately is that you surrender,* moment by moment, *to Who I AM in you.* I want you to walk on earth as you would in heaven. Do as I did when I walked on earth.

My beloved, take time, make time, spend time, *invest time with My FATHER.* Get to know Him personally. Say what He is saying. Do what He is doing. *Your position in life has totally changed.* I AM in you, and you are in the center of Me. You are seated in Me on My Throne next to My FATHER'S throne in heaven. Your position now is in heaven, even as you walk on earth. You are to *look at every situation from My Perspective*. When test, trial, trouble, or sickness comes, look at it with a heavenly perspective. My Promises are a reflection of My Unchanging Nature. In every test, I will reveal My Promises for that situation.

My beloved, trust Me and stay close. Let Me guide you with My Word. Moment by moment, *let Me reveal to you that permission and power* which is able to move you forward through *Intimacy* with Me into your *Identity* in Me so that My *Intent and Purpose* will be fulfilled! Your *Inheritance* and *Impact* will increase in value every day for eternity! My HOLY SPIRIT will show you how to use your personality and your gifts to My FATHER'S Glory!

Declare to your circumstances, "*This promise given to me by GOD is more real than you are! You must now bow to His Promise*"! My beloved, you can say this because you are not being challenged *by* your circumstances or *by* the enemy. The reality is you are actually being challenged *to* believe the promises I have given you in My Word and to believe the provision that I have prepared for you because I AM Good. *Every test is My Opportunity to reveal more of My Goodness to you.* There is absolutely no need for you to focus on anything else. You have a choice: (1) your circumstances are your challenge or (2) you will challenge your circumstances with My Promises.

All of heaven will back you up and move you forward into the territory My FATHER has for you when you respond with the second choice. Your vision and thinking *change* when you focus on My Promises for you. *Expect* that My Resources are your resources. *Learn* that Our Kingdom works differently from how man thinks and works. From above, We *co-labor* with you in your circumstances to bring about the best outcome. Men work from within their circumstances hoping for a better outcome. Our ways are higher than your ways (Isaiah 55:8-9). My FATHER and I love that you are learning to focus on what We am doing with you and learning to focus on where We are taking you through every circumstance, both negative and positive.

Blessing, you bring Us pleasure because you stay in what We say and have said to you, you humbly surrender and receive guidance from HOLY SPIRIT. Therefore, We are able to keep you in your new heavenly position seated in Us—the place from which We operate through you above your circumstances. You are continuing to walk in *your high calling.* You are growing daily in *your new identity.*

As you walk and co-operate with Us, you will *impact* those around you; you will *impact* Our World. Guard your mind from all negativity. Rise up humbly in Our Truth, Love, and Character. You will begin to realize the dreams and vision We have given you as you grow in community where no one is above another. *Blessing, We want you to know that everyone has the same value.* KINGDOM LIVING requires that each person has the same value no matter their education, title, position, or anything else they possess.

Invest your time in *Intimacy* with My FATHER, My HOLY SPIRIT and Me. I want you to walk in the name My FATHER gave you to bless and serve others. This is the *Intended Purpose* for which you were sent to earth. *You know the difference between My Pure Love and counterfeit love. I want you to love with My Love, putting no one above or below you.*

Blessing, as you lift up your generation, enjoying the beauty, the joy, and excitement of letting Me show you how to live on earth as it is in heaven, you will leave a godly *Inheritance* for your descendants and for those that have ears to hear and eyes to see. You will be *My Show and Tell* for the world to experience all of what I did for them on the cross. ***Blessing, J AM showing you how to live a Masterpiece Life of Significance.***

BLESSING speaking to GOD as JESUS

JESUS, I am so grateful and blessed and humbled that *you would use a person who has lived a life of mistakes and failures.* When surrendered to You, I get to practice a life of service in peace, joy, and abundance.

Thank You for putting such great teachers in my life. Melanie Massey is one of those without an awareness that *she is teaching me. I see her humbly walk* in Your HOLY SPIRIT by faith believing Your Word is truth. By watching her response to her mother's health crises, my highest prayer for others changed. Now I know that everything You do in our lives is for our highest good. I learned how to pray with faith from Melanie.

Sometime ago, Melanie's mother, Jin-Jin, had a simple operation on her ankle. After coming home from the hospital, blood clots formed in her heart and in her lungs. She was in ICU for a couple of weeks on life support.

Except to shower, Melanie and her sister Stacy were in the ICU waiting room 24/7. Jin-Jin's doctors were telling them that she was the sickest person in ICU and the doctors did not expect her to live. Melanie put several pictures of Jin-Jin on Facebook. One was a picture of her weeding her flowers; one picture was of her driving her convertible; one was a picture of her at a Mississippi State football game; and lastly, one was a picture of her enjoying her grandchildren.

Melanie asked those of us who knew Jin-Jin to choose a picture of her that jumped out at us. Then we were asked to come in gratitude to You, JESUS, thanking You that her mother would again be doing what she was doing in the picture we chose. I had gone from Ohio to Melanie's home in Louisiana many times. Jin-Jin always picked me up from the airport in her convertible. My picture choice was easy, and I began coming to You with that picture. In my imagination, I placed Jin-Jin in Your Arms on Your Side of the yoke, JESUS.

I held up my side of the yoke by blessing, honoring, worshiping, praising, and thanking You so that You would be glorified in Jin-Jin being able to drive that convertible again. In my imagination and gratitude, I thankfully pictured her picking me up from the airport driving her convertible. I left her in Your hands. My highest prayer for her was my belief that she would drive that convertible again. If Jin-Jin had died, I would have been brokenhearted, but I would have known I had done my part, in faith, to believe in Your Very Best for her. In life or death, I will praise You, JESUS!

This time, You answered *Yes*. Jin-Jin lives and drives that car. Because I love her, I am very grateful! Another time, I might have suffered loss, but what I know is I can trust You JESUS in that everything works out for our good because we have a good, good FATHER!

GOD as JESUS speaking to BLESSING

Beloved, come sit with Me awhile! I want to teach you something very important: *My FATHER, HOLY SPIRIT, and I love to laugh!* What can I say, joy is Who We are. *We want you to laugh in the midst of your circumstances!* Remember, you are made in Our Image. Walk with Us in joy and learn to laugh! We love humor, so joy fills Our Kingdom! *We want you to live in joy on earth as it is in heaven!*

One of our favorite people on earth is Graham Cooke. We love to laugh with him! We love being with him because of his marvelous sense of humor. Sometimes, when I am seriously teaching him something, he spins what I say into something humorous. What he sees and says is *funny,* and I want to laugh, but when I am serious, I want him to pay attention. Because he is humble and faithful to live what I teach him, I love to teach him Who We are, and who We created him to be.

We love that Graham is quick to teach others what I teach him. Because of this, I often talk to him in his dreams. In those dreams, I bring him to heaven to sit high on a hill in a beautiful gazebo surrounded with white flowing curtains he can see through where he sits and waits for me. Normally, I come up the hill holding one of the children and a host of other children walk up the hill with Me.

But in this particular dream, I was very serious about what I had to teach Graham. I came alone. Rather than a warm, kind, and gentle meeting with Graham, I marched up the hill with a very stern look on MY face. Graham knew this dream was different. He saw the stern look on My Face. As I came closer, fear began to creep into his heart.

I walked up to him and said, "Graham, give me back My Stuff!" He responded, "But LORD, I don't know what you mean!" I could tell he was freaking out inside, but again I said even more sternly, "I mean it Graham, give me back My Stuff!" He replied, "Honestly LORD, I don't know what you mean. I have certainly taken only what You have given me, but what 'stuff' are you referring to?"

"Graham, you know you have taken My Stuff. *You have taken fear, depression, issues of abandonment, rejection, hurt, blaming, shaming, condemning, hopelessness, helplessness, greed, jealousy, envy, selfishness, self-seeking, self-righteousness, self-promotion, deceit, intimidation, entitlement, anger, controlling, manipulation, and everything negative. That's Mine!* It's My Stuff! It does not belong to you any longer. Give it back, *now!* I paid a high price for that Stuff on the cross! It is *not* yours anymore, so don't ever try to take it back from Me to use it again! I mean it, Graham! I am serious! No more! Give My Stuff back to Me!"

Blessing, I told you that story so that you would understand that this truth is for you too! *There is a battle for your mind, thoughts, words, attitudes, feelings, deeds, actions, and habits. And I have won that battle once and for all over 2,000 years ago on the cross!* Don't waste your time *refighting* a battle that is not yours to fight! I not only gave you salvation, but I have given you everything you need to *walk freely in My Kingdom on earth as it is in heaven*! I want you to claim the position I bought for you on the cross over two centuries ago!

Negativity, judging, and a "me against others" *mentality* will only make Our world a darker place. Gandhi said it so well, "An eye for an eye will leave everyone blind". There is a big difference between having a different view of a subject and picking a fight. It's truly possible to share our point of view by *shedding light on the subject* rather than participate in *creating more darkness. Your life's purpose now is to be My Example on earth of how life is in heaven.* Stay close to Me. Invest your time with Me. Listen to ME.

Surrender to Me your spirit, mind, will, emotions, body, and silence. Use your words, eyes, arms, hands, and feet directed by My Holy Spirit to bring wisdom, understanding, counsel, power, knowledge and the fear of the Lord (Isaiah 11:2) to your family, to those I bring to you, and to those who receive you as My Messenger. *I want you to pass on My roadmap* for your descendants for one thousand years forward or until My Father sends Me back to earth to rule and reign. *Your purpose is to glorify My Father on earth as He is glorified in heaven!*

BLESSING speaking to GOD as JESUS

JESUS, what excites me most is the opportunity to *uplift my generation!* If a hundred years from now a descendant *researches* my generation, *I want them to know that*, in Your Mercy and Grace, *You used me* to give the world a Roadmap of Your Ways and Kingdom that reveals what you did on the cross for all of us! You taught us to live in our Royal Role and Position high above our earthly circumstances! You taught us to speak Your Heavenly Language to You and with

You as Your Family and Partners co-creating the future You designed for us by using our circumstances for our highest good!

They will find that, before I died on earth, *I had the privilege to practice walking in Your Wisdom, Light, Love, Joy, Grace, High Favor, and Rich Blessing!* They will see how You gave me an inner peace that overflowed with hope, even when at times my heart was breaking. *My family and whoever hears this recorded conversation is also called to uplift their generation for Your Purposes.*

BLESSING speaking to GOD as HOLY SPIRIT

HOLY SPIRIT, moment by moment, day by day, week by week, month by month, year by year, I thank You that You encouraged me to increase in generosity and gratitude! You taught me to give more than I take! You taught me to encourage more than I judge! You taught me to bless more than to curse! You taught me to love more than to hate! You gave me love for The Truth of Your Word!

In Your Word, you gave me an example of David who went out to fight the giant, Goliath, with a slingshot, a few stones and His God, and he took his Goliath down (1 Samuel 17)! This is my template for living! You used David to teach me to use humbly those gifts You have given me while *looking only to My FATHER'S Strength* instead of my vulnerability.

On days when I don't feel equipped, *I know, believe, and declare with thanksgiving* that *You have equipped and empowered me.* Because You only create perfectly and abundantly, and because You abide in my heart and I abide in You, even my worst failures are redeemed as *I surrender all to You*. You are The Source of All Resources in my life. *I am fully resourced* to live humbly as Your Temple and, surrendering all self-sufficiency, *I receive from You!*

I love that I dance more than I sit out the dance as a wallflower. I get to practice being a lamp to light the dark path of others. I get to sing *my song* while inviting others to sing in Your *combined choir*.

Yes, I experience test, trouble, trial, and sickness, but now I know they are not *bad*. Because You are at work, whether seen or unseen, they are *good*. You use each one to elevate me in Your Nature, Truth, and Character. You cause me to love Your Word and Your Guidance because I ask daily for these great gifts. *HOLY SPIRIT, You teach and empower me to humbly help others to enjoy* the Language of Heaven *and humbly encourage them to enjoy living in Your Kingdom.*

Through each struggle, I step into the Image of my heavenly FATHER (Genesis 1:27), seeing with His Eyes and hearing with His Ears. It is very humbling because what I have learned is that *I can respond as He would respond* because of what You have taught me from those struggles which have come into my life. Living aware of Your Presence in me brings curiosity, vibrancy, excitement, joy, expansion, and abundance! Negatives have become opportunities for an upgrade in my soul and for access to all that You have prepared for me!

This year I will live the best year I have ever lived!

But what *really* excites me is that *Your Wisdom, Love, Light, High Favor, and Rich Blessings will flow "through me", not just "to me"! This year is a glorious foundation for the ten-year goal You led Me to set, one year at a time—every year better than the last!* What a glorious life to live, aware that You are in my heart loving and guiding all I do! What a glorious life I live, aware that I am in the center of FATHER GOD'S Son on earth as it is in heaven—abiding, resting, laughing, enjoying being protected from my enemy! I am so grateful to be aware that I rest in the majesty, wisdom, understanding, and knowledge of the Most High GOD, Creator of the universe. I am blessed beyond words! *I now know that my Intent and Purpose no longer exists. I now know that I live <u>Your</u> Intent and Purpose for my life!*

Part Four

INHERITANCE

"I PRESS ON TOWARD THE GOAL
TO WIN THE PRIZE FOR WHICH
GOD HAS CALLED ME HEAVENWARD
IN CHRIST JESUS!"
Philippians 3:14

BLESSING speaking to GOD as JESUS

"When peace like a river attendeth my way, when sorrows like sea billows roll, whatever my lot, Thou hast taught me to say 'It is well, it is well with my soul!'"

JESUS, these words wash over my soul in hard stressful times. When I realize that Horatio Spafford wrote these powerful words immediately after his family had drowned on their trans-Atlantic journey on November 22, 1873, *I want my walk with you to be this deep*. When I would have a tragedy in my life, help me to immediately say, *"It is well, it is well with my soul!"*

JESUS, *it truly astounds me how I remember the darkness of my life before I knew You*. The truth of the sweet words of this hymn did not reflect my life, but they do now. I remember I thought I was smart enough to figure out this life all by myself. I wanted nothing to do with You. I had so much to learn. I had so many places I wanted to see. What I know now is that, when I was going down those different paths, *my soul was actually looking for You. I just didn't know that then*. But after years of unfulfilling paths, my chosen darkness got so dark that, somehow by Your mercy, I was humbled. I had chased all the shiny objects, but none satisfied. How I wish that people would realize, at an earlier age than I did, that our souls are made to rest *in You—that is where our souls long to abide*. That is where the excitement of life dwells.

It was a very dark day of the soul when I began to question myself: "Could I be wrong? Is it possible that there really is a GOD?" I asked aloud: "What do

I have to do? If You are real, can I come as I am?" You so very gently said, "Come to Me" (Matthew 11:28). You didn't say, "Clean up your act, then come see Me". You didn't say, "Do this or that, then come see ME". No, You just simply said, *"Come to ME"*. It was that simple. I remember thinking, *"If You are real, I come"*.

I remember I quickly started reading the Bible. Going to church and reading my Bible, I was still trying to change myself. I began reading the Gospels over and over to see how You lived. I read the *Beatitudes* in Matthew 5 from the Sermon on the Mount that You preached to the disciples and the crowds that sought You. I sincerely studied how You taught them, but I saw little change in me. The words just seemed soothing and beautiful, but unattainable in my fast-paced workplace and world. I went to church for a long time before there was any change in me at all. But, I didn't give up. Once You came into my heart, I felt peace, but *I had no idea how to surrender all to You, Lord.*

When Ellen Stanley was leading her prayer ministry in Indiana, she encouraged me to ask Your HOLY SPIRIT to baptize me. When I asked her how, she offered five steps:

First, thank FATHER GOD that He only gives good gifts;

Second, surrender your spirit in exchange for His HOLY SPIRIT;

Third, ask FATHER GOD to *forgive you for letting another spirit* take HOLY SPIRIT'S place.

Fourth, tell JESUS why you want His HOLY SPIRIT.

Fifth, thank His HOLY SPIRIT for giving you everything that He wants you to have.

Ellen expected me to have a *prayer language* to use to talk with You and told me to expect that Your HOLY SPIRIT would give it to me. After I prayed with her, I did not get a *prayer language*. I just got one syllable: "Zo". So, I just kept praying that one syllable "Zo" over and over day and night. For about a week, I just came to You constantly thanking You for giving me the word "Zo" and a *heavenly* language that I could use to pray. After about a week, I was praying whole sentences with a *language that filled me to overflowing with Your Presence, Peace, and Joy*. You even gave me *heavenly* music and songs to sing to You. There is such wonderful comfort in singing to You when circumstances are hard in my life.

Lord JESUS, after Your HOLY SPIRIT *filled, permeated, and surrounded me completely*, it was as though the Sermon on the Mount *exploded* for me. Your HOLY SPIRIT brought one of the Beatitudes to mind in a particular circumstance. Initially, I was very uncomfortable. I felt real discomfort. I was faced with responding in my old natural way or *being open to responding in the new way I felt You were teaching, leading, and empowering me to respond.*

Lord JESUS, *at first* when I surrendered to Your HOLY SPIRIT, *Your Way felt strict and hard.* Little by little, *I committed more time* to *hearing* Your Voice in Your Word *and speaking with You* in prayer. I started with 30 minutes a day. *It was so hard to stay focused that long.* But after a while, *something wonderful happened*—I found I didn't want to leave the place of supernatural peace I had discovered. I began to gradually notice that my conversations were becoming more and more like Your responses to my circumstances. I discovered it was a process that required *making You first in my life before Your HOLY SPIRIT could have His Way in me.*

It *amazed* me that I began to see the negative things that happened to my family and me from a heavenly perspective. I actually started to find myself *celebrating* because I was experiencing a feeling of being *lifted* up to higher levels in Your SPIRIT. I found out that it is Your HOLY SPIRIT'S task to *conform* me to *Your Image.* It has become my daily experience to live on earth as Your ambassador. I am seeing more and more of Your Character and Humility where I've never seen it before. Your HOLY SPIRIT has used those things that would have naturally made me anxious, stressed and depressed to set me free. Now, more and more, *I feel like my soul is free to soar!*

GOD as JESUS speaking to BLESSING

Beloved, *this is the "Road Map" My FATHER gave you to leave for your descendants*: First, _commit_ to build _Intimacy_ with FATHER, HOLY SPIRIT and ME, making Us your First Love. Second, _ask_ My FATHER the new name He calls you so that you can walk in your new _Identity._ Third, _discover_ My FATHER'S _Intent_ for your life and learn the purpose for which He created you. Fourth, _receive_ the exciting _Inheritance_ My FATHER has prepared to give to and through you. Fifth, _expect_ to _Impact_ earth and populate heaven with the life My FATHER has planned for you.

My HOLY SPIRIT will teach you how to give more in order to receive more. You will *uplift your generation* as He leads you and then your descendants will experience you as more fully alive as you age. I will teach you to *walk in True, Pure, and Heavenly Love*. It will become easier for them to uplift their generations directed by Me *because* of *your example*. When they see you *practice, fail, correct, rise, struggle, succeed, repeat*—all done *with Joy*—they will believe that intentional living produces a *significant life*. I will teach you how to live *My Roadmap*, which will *lead you farther, further, and to My FATHER*. I will teach you how to glorify My FATHER in all you do.

When others look at your life, I want them to see that *the Hope you've placed in Me is real*, that it is *well placed*, and that it is able to produce *desirable results*. When you are unable to speak *to* Me or *for* Me, My HOLY SPIRIT will speak *for you through you*. I speak with sounds that *express what words cannot*; My Sounds *replace* your words—I can work through a wail, a cry, a sigh, or even silence because it is your heart that I hear. You are again like an Infant, *a Child depending on your Perfect FATHER*, and that is a very good thing (Romans 8:22-27).

Come to Me with the same excitement a child has at Christmas. I AM free to respond to My Perfect Will for you. When I work on your behalf, My HOLY SPIRIT brings all good things to you, and to the rest of My Family.

As FATHER, Son, and HOLY SPIRIT, *We have had a plan that has worked for generations and is still working* for HOLY SPIRIT to guide you to become just like Me. We designed this plan from before the foundations of the world. *We have always desired A Family On Earth like this*, from design, to speaking into being, to sustaining, to making right, and to sharing My Glory! *It delights Us to show up and show out in and through each of you!* That's that—no one can argue with *Us*—you can only agree with Us that *We are TOTALLY for you, and that no one and nothing can prevail against you!* I gave you everything when I gave you Myself. Then, by My HOLY SPIRIT, My FATHER placed you in Me and Me in you! (Romans 8:28-30)

speaking into being, to sustaining, to making right, and to sharing My Glory! *It delights Us to show up and show out in and through each of you!* That's that—no one can argue with *Us*—you can only agree with Us that *We are TOTALLY for you, and that no one and nothing can prevail against you!* I gave you everything when I gave you Myself. Then, by My HOLY SPIRIT, My FATHER placed you in Me and Me in you! (Romans 8:28-30)

No one and nothing can stand against you because of *what My FATHER has done through Me on the cross. My dying and rising totally in His Power placed Me in the transformational turning point of History and placed Me intentionally in the position of My authority as King of kings and Lord of lords.* It will sound strange to you, but We talk *about you* all day long and speak *Our Plan for you* into being. We created you to overcome everything that comes your way while you live on earth. You are part of a long line who is only as vulnerable as *the conquering Mighty Warrior I AM. No one and nothing can separate you from My Everlasting Love!* (Romans 8:31-39)

GOD as FATHER speaking to BLESSING

Remember the night when I woke you up out of a sound sleep? You sat straight up in bed. It is the first time I had ever spoken to you in that way. I laugh as I remember that night. You were shocked because you had never experienced Me in that way. I told you that before you die, I wanted you to *write a book* that I would speak into you. I said it was to be *a Roadmap for your descendants for a thousand years forward or until I send My Son back to earth*. It is for you and your family, but *it is also for all who have ears to hear and eyes to see*. I also told you to start a *non-profit* before you die, but that time has not yet come.

BLESSING speaking to GOD as FATHER

FATHER, I get it! I chose to believe You and now I understand that it isn't just me, my family, my generation, and my descendants, but it is also all those who are willing to see and hear *Your Intent and Purpose* for them and their descendants for a thousand years forward. Also, with Your eyes, I see family enjoying reunions together giving seminars for each other to share what they have learned about *Intimacy* with You, and how You are transforming their lives. My life as Blessing is my *ceiling*, but it is as the *floor* of Your Vision for my family and for every reader who will take *Our* conversation as *theirs. I want my ceiling to be the floor for others* to be more intimate with You than I have been; I want others to walk in who You created them to be more than I have walked in who You created me to be; I want others to live their *Intent and Purpose* more fully than I have lived my *Intent and Purpose;* I want them to leave a deeper godly *Inheritance* than I have left; I want them to *Impact* earth and heaven more than I have.

GOD as JESUS speaking to BLESSING

One of the most important things for you to do is *practice what you are already doing*. Each morning, you recognize that I AM the One Who causes you to open your eyes for that day. Blessing, when I bring your family members and others into your life that day, you recognize that I have brought them to cause *My Blessings* to flow *through* you *to* them. Remember, *I bless you to bless others*. You are My 'Show and Tell' of how I want My Family to live! Moment by moment, I want you to practice *humility and surrender* while receiving from Me, My Wisdom, Understanding, Counsel, Power, Knowledge, and Fear of The Lord (Isaiah 11:2).

My beloved Blessing, this is so important because it is the way to *throw satan off of his game plan* for you. He never gives up. While you are *aware* of him, *your focus must always be on Me*. Remember, when he raises his head to kill, steal and destroy, begin to *celebrate how I will bless you for his attack*. Fear not. Every attack means more blessing for you. Live daily aware of Us together—*you are in Me and I AM in you*! To the *degree and depth* he *steals* from you, I will *reward* you more than seven fold (Proverbs 6:31).

I have used your conversations with My servant Mark to *raise the way you value your conversation with Me. Prayer* is vital—it is life-sustaining—it *causes you to thrive*. By prayer, I want you to *persevere and war with My weapons*. Nothing can stand against you. I have made you strong in My Strength. All *Our enemies must bow* before My Father. They *must run* or *be destroyed*. I don't lift *them* up. I lift *you* up into authority over them. They lose heart when *I reveal Myself through you* (Psalm 18:46-50).

Remember, how I spoke to you through Mark about how *I AM your Rock-solid Foundation. You have every reason to praise Me* all around the world among the nations I have established. Be determined to praise, exalt, and worship Me as I send you to them! My unfailing kindness will be shown to you because My FATHER has chosen you to be My family forever!

My beloved, I tell you again, what I told you then, you will not stray from *My instructions* because you have learned to listen for *My Voice.* Hear Me. *Respond* by obeying My Voice to bypass consequences. Your motives are purified by My HOLY SPIRIT. By My Grace, your *right-doing* flows out of your *right-being* in Me (Proverbs 19:27–29).

Remember, We talked about what My HOLY SPIRIT wrote through My servant Oswald: how it is *the Presence of My* HOLY SPIRIT *in you that makes you right* in your dreams and in places within your mind that you do not *consciously control.* Just *recognizing Him and coming to Me* is doing your part in *Our Partnership.* I will work in and through you. Ultimately, all there is for you to do is *yield* yourself to Me, and all there is for Me to do is *manifest* Who I AM. Mark Williams explained the struggle My children have with learning that obedience does not make them pure. My HOLY SPIRIT alone makes you pure and manifests My Purity in you. As you recognize and acknowledge Me, you see that I AM Truth, and that I AM My Word present and alive in you to accomplish what I have promised! I give you My DNA, My Nature in exchange for yours. *I want to be Myself in you!*

Blessing, ten years ago before you even knew what it meant, I instructed Toby (My beloved Messenger and Missionary) to email you a Promise from My Word that I spoke over you and your descendants. *I now also give that same Promise to all who have ears to hear and eyes to see.* The words were written as Isaiah 54:2–3 ESV:

> "Enlarge the place of your tent, stretch your tent curtains wide.
> Do not hold back.
> Lengthen your cords, strengthen your stakes, for you will spread out to the right and to the left.
> Your descendants will possess the nations, and settle in the desolate cities."

My Friend, *your time has come.* You and Charlie have sought Me and found Me. *You have pleased My FATHER because of your faith, because you believe that He exists, and that He rewards those who earnestly seek Him* (Hebrew 11: 6). Yes My dear Child, you and Charlie have found My FATHER. You seek My Face, and you have found Me (Psalm 27:8).

BLESSING speaking to GOD as JESUS

JESUS, *I have sought You and found You* in Your Word. The love of FATHER GOD has been shed abroad in my heart by the HOLY SPIRIT, and His Love abides in me richly. I keep myself in the Kingdom of Light and in Your Word. The wicked one touches me not. I fear not for GOD has given me His Spirit of Power, of Love, and of a Sound Mind. No weapon formed against me shall prosper. Every tongue that rises against me shall be shown to be wrong. You are on my side. I tread upon and over all the power of the enemy. I take Your Shield of Faith to quench every fiery dart. Greater are You within me than the one who is in the world (Psalm 91:13, Isaiah 54:17, Romans 5:5, Romans 8:31, Ephesians 6:16, 2 Timothy 1:7, John 4:4, John 4:16, John 5:18).

Master, You were so kind to me when You taught me the important principle of *More Than Enough vs. Never Enough* through my good friend Brian Russell when I read his blog. He is a leader of leaders. He simplified principles he learned from Michael Hyatt and brilliantly condensed their reality like this:

Abundance thinkers believe there is always more than enough where that came from. Abundance thinkers share their knowledge, contacts, and compassion with others. Abundance thinkers default to trust and build rapport easily. Abundance thinkers welcome competition; believing the pie will always grow.

Scarcity thinkers believe there will never be enough. Scarcity thinkers are stingy with their knowledge, contacts, and compassion. Scarcity thinkers default to suspicion and find it difficult to build rapport. Scarcity thinkers resent competition, believing pies become smaller; they weaken.

JESUS, I used to ask myself: "How can I *get by with less* than is expected? Why am I so *pessimistic* about the future? Why do I always believe that *tough times are ahead*? Why do I think so *small* and avoid risk at all cost? Why do I feel *entitled* and at the same time always feel *fearful*?

JESUS, I ask myself: "How can I *give more* than is expected? Am I *optimistic* about the future You have created for me? Do I believe the *best is yet to come*? Do I trust You enough to think *big* and embrace risk? Am I *thankful* for and *confident* in what You have prepared for Me, but do not see?

Beloved Teacher, You have shown me that what I wrote was so important for my family and all who have ears to hear and eyes to see. Just as Michael taught Brian, I realize more and more that what I *think* creates my reality more than I ever thought possible. It is You Who have taught me to *guard* my heart and mind. You have taught me that my negative *thoughts* have the ability to *delay the plan You have for me* and my positive thoughts have the ability to *accelerate* Your plan.

You have *spoken this conversation* into my mind *to form and shape it into this book*. Like the words from Brian's blog, again and again, you show me the exact place where something fits in this book. The pieces continue to appear to show up without my asking. Some days it was scripture, some days a story, some days a quote from a post or article or blog. *Each day You gave me exactly what I was to write*. I am grateful that You continue to pour rivers of living water through me!

You have given scriptures to me that speak always of victory, of joy, and of abundance. I will take responsibility for all mistakes in this book, but You, sweet JESUS, have graciously given my family and those who have ears to hear and eyes to see the *Five Gifts That Create Legacy.*

On this mountain I am climbing, things are now so different. Where there was darkness, now there is light. Where there was pain, now there is healing. Where there was rejection, now there is acceptance. Where there was hatred, now there is love.

This is a different kind of love than I have known for most of my life. What I experience now is a love that is *the pure holy love of heaven* here on earth. It *is a love that . . .*

> *never gives up,*
> *doesn't want what it doesn't have,*
> *doesn't strut,*
> *doesn't have a swelled head,*
> *doesn't force itself on others,*
> *isn't always "me first",*
> *doesn't fly off the handle,*
> *doesn't keep score on the sins of others,*
> *doesn't revel when others grovel,*
> *takes pleasure in the flowering of truth,*
> *puts up with anything,*
> *trust GOD always,*
> *always looks for the best,*
> *never looks back,*
> *keeps going to the end.*
> *(1 Corinthians 13)*

JESUS, You are always on time! To teach me more about *Your Pure Love,* you brought *four very special people* into my life in *Pittsburgh*: Amy, Sierra, Jim, and Yolande. I learned anew to die to self. I learned you must give generously in order to be able to receive fully. I learned that, through the cross, *You have made it possible for all of us to be on the same level with You JESUS*—none above, none below. *I learned to love with an open heart.* I learned the words of each person are as important as the words of every other person. I learned that *Your Pure Love is truly beautiful* when *shared in community* with others.

It seems too *good* to be true, and yet it *is* true. My spirit burns with *a passion to show the world* that even the painful parts of life are good. It is *all good.*

I love where I am on this mountain. It doesn't surprise You that *this is the best part of my journey.* The sun is warm on my back, and the air up here is sweetly refreshing. *From this place, everything seems possible.* I see other people who are in the twilight of their own journey. Looking closely, the difference is clear: they are living in fear of falling off of this mountain, and they look at me wondering why *I am so full of hope and peace and energy?* Their eyes say: "Help me! I'm falling!" When they know what You have taught me, they too can have what You've given me!

My heart leaps with expectancy over *the possibilities of igniting a fire that will light their path and cause them to see deep treasures within them that finally bring them rest and peace.* As I climb, I look back and I know I want to lend a hand to those who are just starting, to those who are in the middle, and to those who are near the end of their journey.

As we climb together, we gather passion. We delight to sing our own song while inviting others to sing in our choir. Catalysts together, we unite with delight to see each person discover *Five Gifts of INTIMACY,*

IDENTITY, INTENT, INHERITANCE, and IMPACT that You long to give them! We delight that You provide the Pure Love in Us that sets the environment for each one to find and fulfill the destiny You have prepared for them before You spoke the universe into existence!

We are a blessed people because we are friends. We have a *common cause to reproduce and gather an army* of climbers from diverse backgrounds, experiences and ages that are blind to prejudice and overcoming circumstances. Soaring over complex situations, we share with others the *strategic effective keys* that we have *accessed and used* to *unlock acute* pain to *heal chronic* pain.

We train a group of climbers whom You have called to understand with clarity the *Intent and Purpose* for which they were born! Their *souls burn with a passion to have a greater impact* on the world around them. Each of them is amazed as they recognize that they are on a very personal and special path, which You designed for them as the Master Planner. As *individuals* recognize their own purpose, *relationships* are healed and *marriages* are transformed.

Together, Charlie and I share *a desire and dream to create an environment* where *marriage is truly honored the way FATHER created it to be* and *truly demonstrated the way You love your Church as Your Bride*. We want to create a *safe place* where we teach other climbers how to experience a relationship bathed in Your Pure Love. We see the *false counterfeit love* that manipulates and controls so many relationships. It *breaks our hearts and we know it breaks Yours*. It takes some time to build relationships on Your Foundation of Pure Love.

Charlie and I are eager to teach energized husband climbers how to create an environment where *wife climbers feel Secure, Cherished, and Important,* and teach motivated wife climbers how to create an environment where *husband climbers feel Respected, Empowered, and Confident.*

Teach them through us how to *speak* to a person *with honor and respect,* instead of dishonor and disrespect out of their own pain. We have learned the hard way to *become real and transparent.* We know You will teach them through us the *joy* of knowing how to *connect heart to heart* and communicate better than ever before!

Charlie and I have responded to Your Voice calling us to fulfill the *Intent and Purpose* for which we were born. We now have access to reach our potential in our marriage and in all of our relationships. *We long to know how amazing our marriage and relationships can be! We long to take others with us beyond the limits of our imagination into the Inheritance we dream of leaving to those who follow us!*

JESUS, Your HOLY SPIRIT now calls out through us to others who will join us in the army of Your followers to become extraordinary climbers on this very special mountain. You offer to us the privilege to bring the Kingdom of heaven to earth. You paid for this privilege with Your Blood. We bring with us the ingredients to customize our *Inheritance* and upgrade the quality of our *Impact.* We know *You understand the treasure* of our *Legacy* is at stake.

Our hope is that each climber enjoys an exhilarating experience and a breathtaking view! Jesus *You promise to empower each climber* to reach its summit.

The sweet fragrance of Your Presence refreshes the atmosphere like the river filled with the Water of Life, clear and crystal flowing from the throne of GOD and of the LAMB, by which climbers yield fruit continuously, and the leaves of their lives are for the healing of the nations.

Come, dear climbers, to this very special mountain where your walk with JESUS inspires a GODLY inheritance for your descendants to follow.

GOD as JESUS speaking to YOU

Hear Me, Child . . . I <u>AM</u> *calling* <u>YOU!</u>

Part Five

IMPACT

"DON'T BE AFRAID, FOR I AM WITH YOU.
DO NOT BE DISMAYED, FOR I AM
YOUR GOD
I WILL STRENGTHEN YOU. I WILL
HELP YOU.
I WILL UPHOLD YOU WITH MY
VICTORIOUS RIGHT HAND."
Isaiah 31:10

BLESSING speaking to GOD as JESUS

JESUS, here We are finishing this portion of many years of conversation with infinitely more conversation to go! Here We are writing the last piece of the book You have been writing through me. I feel a little sad. These last months, You and I have spent all day consciously together in companionship and conversation—I, in an attitude of rather amazing worship while You have been busy orchestrating every page through me. It has been *LIFE CHANGING!*

Right now, I feel the *Fire of Your Presence* in my heart. I am so humbled. Your Presence has burned in my heart for much of this past month. Because of Your Fire burning in my chest, I feel so connected to Your Disciples who walked with You on the road to Emmaus. After You left them, they said "Did not our heart burn while He talked with us on the road, and while He opened the Scriptures for us?" (Luke 24:32) What amazes me is that *You are the same* yesterday, today, and forever (Hebrews 13:8)! I know because of Your Word *that was then,* and *this is now . . .* the same! I feel the same Fire of Your Presence in my heart those two disciples felt on the road to Emmaus!

When I first *became aware* my heart was burning, I was *undone!* Inwardly, I became *very quiet, without words.* Silence was the *only* response I had to *offer* You. I could only bow before You, humbled beyond words. I am so grateful *You are so available to me* and to *us.* All it takes is our *willingness* to be *available* to You. I believe this time and experience has come through staying at Your Feet morning, noon and night as I wrote the conversation that is this book. I don't want to *lose this closeness,* Lord JESUS! I *know* I can *trust* You because You don't *change!* We will still be this close, if *I don't* move away. I just *want* more and more of You! Lord JESUS, keep me faithful! I want to discover more of Who You are, what Your Word has yet to teach me about who I am in You, how I can love YOU more, and how I can love others more with Your Perfect Love. That is *still my Task!*

It is as though You are daily giving me a deeper peel of the onion to know what has always been true! Ifs not about knowing *about* You. It's about really knowing You by *personally* experiencing Your Holy Love! You are *intimately* with *each* of us *every* moment! We have *no* relationship that *compares* to this. And yet, so often, we simply are not aware enough to know that. I hear You say You will shed *Your Holy Light,* even into the pit of our deepest darkness. Every one of us has our own journey, and You are there with each of us. It remains our choice to accept *Your invitation* to *walk with* and *follow* You. We *choose* just *how close* that walk will be! Without even being aware, we decide the amount of distance that exists between You and us. Yet, even in that, I hear You say to me that *each moment is Holy and ordained for our highest good.*

How sad You must be JESUS when we choose to put on *masks of religion* over accepting Your offer of a *face to face* relationship with You! We often judge others without first walking in their shoes. We think we know You better than others do. We say we love You, yet our actions are full of prejudice, arrogance, pride, and condescension. We gossip to make us feel better about ourselves. The list goes on and on. We think we have to *do something for You* rather than *be with*

You experiencing Your Presence, hearing Your Voice, knowing Your Ways, following Your Lead, discerning Your Wisdom, and enjoying Your Peace.

JESUS, I *can't believe* that I *actually laughed* the other day when You said to me, "Blessing, I don't need you. I really don't need you. I *want* you, but I don't *need* you." JESUS, this touched something inside me *so deep that I cannot explain.* I became completely overwhelmed by the reality that You *don't* need me, but *You* really *want me.* This Truth has finally come home to me, and it *means the world* to me!

Then, when 1 thought there couldn't be more, You revealed the depth of what You have been teaching me and I found myself saying: "Yes, Lord JESUS, it has taken many years, but finally You have made me realize *the privilege of hearing Your Voice,* being *guided* by You, *saying* what *You say,* and *doing* what *You do!* And *Oh precious JESUS*—Yes, I get that wrong a lot, but You are amazingly gracious patient, and kind to me! You let me know once again that *practice has not ended* and, because of You, *I can never fail the test!* You present my tests again and again *until I pass* each one. *YOU are more compassionate than anyone else I know!* Your Loving kindness never fails!

You are patient, and kind to me! You let me know once again that *practice has not ended* and, because of You, *I can never fail the test!* You present my tests again and again *until I pass* each one. *YOU are more compassionate than anyone else I know!* Your Loving kindness never fails!

Wow! *What is amazingly humbling is to know You.* not just to know something about You! Blown away, that's how I am when I think of how very profound, yet so simple that is. When I first began to *move toward* You, I started to read the Bible. I read about the strange creatures around Your Throne in heaven with eyes all over their body. I read they constantly say the words "Holy, Holy, Holy". It "weirded me out.". Now I think, I may be beginning to "get it", at least a little bit. They are still so completely *overwhelmed* with the dimensional *magnitude* of the width, length, height, and depth of Your Pure Perfect Powerful Love that they have *no other words to say* but *"HOLY."* You are so much more than *extravagantly* generous! I am learning that, no matter whatever or however much I give to You, I can never *out give* you! *Whatever I possess that You want from me is Yours!*

You always surprise me with Your Gifts which are *always* much bigger and more important than what I have *ever* given You. My *favorite* gift from You so far is *my heart burning with Your Presence.* Tears are in my eyes right now as my heart burns again! Just to be in Your Presence right now, I am undone!

You are greater . . .
You are higher . . .
You are sweeter . . .
You are wiser . . .
You are power . . .
You are knowledge . . .
You are Savior . . .
You are Redeemer
You are Friend . . .
You are *The First Son* of many sons!

You were there during the Depression when I was born at home with the help of a family friend who happened to be a doctor. You were there at the first breath of the person who is reading this book. *The One Who* spoke the cosmos into being, the Creator of the sun and moon, the Master *Designer of the star* was actually with each of us at the moment of our first breath. *You were always there!*

You were there for all of *our Firsts*! Our first sight, our first touch, our first embrace, our first steps! You were there the first time we fell off a bike or out of a tree, lost a brother in the grocery store or lost a brother who ran out into a street without looking. You were always there!

You were *there* when we went to high school or didn't; when we made the football team or didn't. You were there when in high school I first experienced the symptoms of multiple sclerosis or didn't. You were there when I had an abortion or didn't. You were there when I flunked out of school, and when I went to prison. You were there when I made the honor roll, and when I spoke at graduation to 1,500 students. You were always there!

You *were* there when I went to college or didn't. You were there when the first love of my life died of cancer or didn't. You were there when I could not get a boyfriend, and when I did. You were there when 1 my boyfriend abused me, and when I had a boyfriend who didn't. You were there when I drank too much, and when I refused to drink. You were there when I got my first job, and when I lost it. You were always there!

You were at my wedding and at the birth of each child. You were there when I was unable to have a child. You were there when we adopted each child. You were there when my parents divorced and when they didn't.

You were there when 1 was diagnosed with Multiple Sclerosis. You were there when I was so depressed that I wanted to give up and die. You were always there!!!

You were *there* through those horrible years of physical pain, seizures, and unable to drive. You were there with me when half my body, half my tongue, half my esophagus were numb, and when the room would spin so much that even being on the bed was too much movement. You were there each time I threw a pillow on the floor, holding my head for hours at a time.

Yes, You *were* there when I was in a wheel chair. You were there in the class when Neil Anderson's book *Victory Over Darkness* was taught. You were there with me when I prayed the prayers in the back of Neil's second book *The Bondage Breaker* with his wife JoAnn. You were always there!

Yes and Hallelujah, *You* were there four hours later when *every* symptom left me—that was over 20 years ago in 1994. You were there for two years when a symptom would try to come back over me. You reminded me how my body felt with no symptoms. When a symptom would try to come back, I ran to YOU. This was a *real testing time,* and You taught me how to declare Your Promises. You taught me how to do *warfare* with the enemy. After two years, all the symptoms went away until last year when one tried to resurface. You were *always* there!

I have learned the enemy *never* gives up. Last year, I started to get very dizzy. It was so bad I had to lie down on the bed. I just held my head still for two hours. It took that long before I became aware and said "Oh my word! That is the same symptom I had in 1994, only then the dizziness was so bad I had to throw a pillow on the floor and hold my head still for hours. It felt the same, just not so severe. My enemy was too sly to make it bad enough that I would throw the pillow on the floor. If he had done that, I would have quickly recognized what he was up to. As it was, it took me two hours of this nonsense to realize it was the same. I simply said, "Oh, get out of here". Immediately, all of the dizziness was gone. You were *always* there!!!

Imagine, the enemy waited 23 years to put an MS symptom back on me. The enemy is very patient. He has been around for centuries, a long time. He knows you, and, he knows me. He knows the weak spots of each individual, and he knows the weaknesses of our families. *Generationally,* he knows each family's weak spots. He will even skip a *generation* and come to our children or grandchildren. He never gives up, but *his generational schemes are as easily undone as his short term escapades.* We need to be aware that *You, JESUS were always there, and You are always here where we are!*

You were there when I spent so many years going to church thinking I knew what it was to honor You with my life. You knew better, yet You were there. Finally, You removed *deception* from my mind, eyes, and heart that made me think I could be good *enough on my own* to serve You. I am so grateful You taught me that was a lie. I will never be able to be *good enough on my own* to serve You. You said that only GOD is good (Mark 10:18). But then, I remembered Your Word says that FATHER GOD made me righteous by what You did for Me on the cross many years ago (2 Corinthians 5:21). You *were* always there *for me.*

You were there thirteen years ago *when 1 was 70 years old.* I was speaking to You in prayer when I said to You: "Sweet JESUS, when Your disciples asked You how to pray, You said *"Thy* will be done on earth as it is in heaven". Looking back *from age 83,* a 70 year old looks like *a young chick* to me. But, honestly, I thought I *was* old back *then*—having maybe four or five years left. With time so short, I didn't think I was asking for too much. In those *transformational* moments, *You were purposely there!*

I remember like it was yesterday when I said to You: "JESUS, as I look around, even in the church, I don't see people living on earth as it is in heaven, even though You taught Your disciples to pray for this. I want to please You. Before I die, I want to use up all the gifts You have given me on earth as they are in heaven. Would You be so kind as to give me the gift of showing me how Blessing would live if I lived on earth as it is in heaven ? Would You give me that gift for the rest of my life?"

You were always there!

JESUS, I will tell people this Truth: "Don't ask GOD to show you what you would look like on earth as it is in heaven *unless* you are *willing* to turn *everything* over to GOD. It is through the tests, troubles, trials and sicknesses that we learn to trust that GOD is right *there at the point of our pain.* He doesn't cause these things, but oh how great He is at using them to teach *us faith—to put our belief and trust into action!* He causes us to know Him, His Promises, and His Provision through each trial." *You are always there!*

JESUS, it seems as though in the hard times, FATHER GOD will let me walk right to the edge of a high cliff. If I take one more step I will be destroyed. The valley below is deep and rocky. At the edge of this cliff, it seems as if You are saying, "Will you trust Me even here?" When I put myself in unhealthy situations from less than stellar decision making, You are right there to bring me back. No matter how bruised, battered or desperate 1 am. You pick me up. I sit humbly at Your Feet again, and You give me Your Wisdom, Understanding, Counsel, Power, Knowledge, and Holy Fear of the LORD (Isaiah 11:2). *You are always there!*

You've allowed me these experiences often enough that I've learned something very important. It brings me such peace to have this understanding from You: *I can always trust You.* That is a given. You never change. What I have learned through many trials is that You have to be able to trust me. When the enemy attacks, You now actually laugh at his attempts to get me down. You consistently use the hard things to teach me how to go to a deeper, sweeter walk with You. I hear You saying "*Trust Me*". *You are always there!*

GOD as JESUS speaking to BLESSING

Blessing, I AM always making intercession for you *to My FATHER* in heaven *(Hebrew 7:25), and HOLY SPIRIT is* interceding for you *on* earth *(Romans 8:26).* When you join Us in what We are praying, we become a three-stranded cord that cannot be easily broken *(Ecclesiastes 4:12).* Blessing, We want you to be aware before you pray! We want you to listen, then ask US what *We* are praying about this situation. Write the words down We give you, and then join Us in how We are praying.

We love that you *believe Us.* When you pray what we are praying, We *answer* and you *see* the Glory of

GOD (John 11:40). "Ask and it will be given to you, seek and you will find, knock and it will be opened to you. Everyone who asks receives, and the one who seeks finds, and to the one who knocks it will be opened." (Matthew 7:7)

Practice rejoicing first Blessing, Praise and worship Our FATHER with confidence and boldness, expecting and thanking Him that He is Good, He is Kind, and He is for you. He intends for you to *prosper in every situation. Replace* anxiety with expectancy and thanksgiving. After you begin your prayers joyfully and expectantly, there will come a time you will know when to be quiet. You will feel the Presence of FATHER God. Then stop to listen, because often He speaks in a word or a phrase, and if you listen to hear not to respond, you will hear enough words to form a simple prayer. *Write* out a few sentences. This way, you are *joining* Us, and you will be *praying in agreement with* Us, not *up to* Us. You will *transcend your problems* and *leave meager possibilities behind.* You will grow into living in abundance. Be anxious for nothing (Philippians 4:6-7). We *are* always there!

My beloved, take this more seriously than you are now. I want you to *make a plan to be better at living in rejoicing* by this time next year. *I Learn* to leap for joy always in every circumstance (both good and bad). *Make* all circumstances the same for you whether negative or positive because to Us they are. To Us, both are the same because both are opportunities. You were created in Our Image (Genesis 1:27), so rejoicing over all circumstances gives you a chance to *practice walking in Our Image.* It is HOLY SPIRIT'S *Joyful Task* to teach you and guide you to respond as I do. My FATHER and I *are* love! Plan to keep on practicing joy and *expect* that We will give you *an upgrade*. Watch Us work in your circumstances to give you High Favor and Rich Blessings. Be persistent Sometimes *Our FATHER just enjoys Himself when* He experiences your *trust,* your *belief,* your *voice,* and your *passion.* He *always* hears *you, without fail.* That is *Who* We are. Communicating with you is not a chore, *it is Our delight[1]*. We are always with you— *closer* than the air you breathe!

BLESSING speaking to GOD as JESUS

Wow! JESUS, *this is what I mean* when I say living in Your HOLY SPIRIT. You make life better and better every day! I am living in Kingdom living. What a *privilege* to *rest* in You JESUS, and *practice* Your Ways! I want to share something with You for my benefit, Charlie's benefit, the benefit of our children and grandchildren, and the benefit of those who have ears to hear and eyes to see. Yes, I laugh thinking You must get bored because You already know how it everything ends. But, *I ask You to richly bless everyone reading this conversation* (which is now a book) with Your strength, *and* reveal *to them the joy that there is* not a more rewarding prayer *to pray than* "Lord JESUS, teach me how to walk on earth as it is in heaven"!

Precious JESUS, to *everyone* reading I say, "Be very brave! Do not be afraid!" With everything in me, I *encourage* you to pray: "Lord JESUS, teach me how to walk on earth as it is in heaven" and really *mean* it. *You will not be sorry, not ever.* It is the most *honest* and bravest thing I have *ever* done. *Why* do you need to be brave? Perhaps, your experience will be different than my experience. Since GOD never does things twice the same way, I'm sure yours will not be identical.

For me, although these have been the *hardest* years of my life, they have also been the *most glorious* years of my life. *Every year* my life gets better and *better,* sweeter and *sweeter!* JESUS, You are very *active and alive* in me to clean out the things in me that are not of You. You are *working* on me from the inside out, not from the outside in. You are always *there!*

At age 83 and as long as I have been a Christian, you would think I would feel *shame* about *the ugly stuff that has been in me,* but *You have taught me to give thanks for and to celebrate all things.* I sincerely thank You because I know that, *"whatever that thing is",* it *must go before I can have more of You.* I laugh and say to You "Thank You FATHER, I know! I know! And I am so grateful to have "this thing" gone because *now I get more of You!"* You are always *there!*

I rejoice with a *joy* that is *totally undeniable, unexplainable, and unparalleled.* I have *no enemies.* People can hate me, but *I am compelled to love them back because JESUS does.* Yes, I will *never* have an enemy! Yes, these last years *have been* the hardest yet most glorious years of my life. But, *how* can that be true? *Hardest—Glorious?* I believe that is *how* FATHER GOD *works.* It's *His Way* with *His best friends.* When I look at Job, his experience with both his friends, and with GOD, I think now there is *one blessed man!*

Job had a *grand* life! He had a life when *everything* was going his way and *nothing* seemed too difficult (Job 2:28). Then *everything* was taken away and things were *beyond tough* for a long time. Job could see *no* light, and his friends *judged* him. Yet, *our faithful FATHER never left him, and Job never left GOD.*

I have *learned* to *rejoice in testing* (James 1) *because* You have made known to me the example of *Chinese Christians* who do this so beautifully. I so admire them. They are the underground Christian church in China. They stand on the *Five Pillars of Truth:*

Pillar 1: *PRAY TO* GOD—First and most important, listen to Jesus, then talk to Jesus.

Pillar 2: *KNOW* HIS WORD—Find Intimacy with God through His Word.

Pillar 3: *PREACH* HIS WORD—Everyone verbalizes the Gospel to others day and night.

Pillar 4: *EXPECT* HIS MIRACLES—Expect miracles from God every week.

Pillar 5: *EMBRACE* HIS SUFFERING—Be grateful to be worthy of sharing His suffering and glory.

JESUS, I know *You know* that, if everything was smooth and positive for us all the time, we would *never lean* into the things of GOD. Although you cannot, I wish you, the reader, could have walked with me through my last thirteen years with GOD. It has been glorious! You know *why my endless praise is insufficient.*

JESUS, I want to share with those reading our conversation a few snap shots of my experiences with You, FATHER GOD, and HOLY SPIRIT during these last thirteen years.

As strange as it may sound, this really happened to me. FATHER GOD would speak to me by *using my mind,* but I knew I was not *thinking* the thoughts that were coming into my mind. It *does sound* weird—but I know only GOD could do that (satan could only influence my thoughts). But with *His Pure Perfect Love, GOD taught me how* to *use* the *Blood, Name, and Resurrection Power of JESUS* to *shut down* satan, his fallen angels, and his plan for my day and night. It's that *simple,* just *say* it and they *have* to obey. You were always *there!*

Back in 2004, FATHER GOD first told me to start a *"GOD—BLESSING Journal"* for each year going forward. I was to *write to Him using black ink* and His *response to me was to be in red ink. I still do that* for eleven months out of the year and have always been grateful for His *specific* instructions to me. Then, I take the entire month of December to *review* that year with GOD. I am unable to *adequately explain* to you how *wonderful* it is to see *the faithfulness* of GOD as I re-read what He has taught me during that year. He told me that when I told someone I would pray for them I was to put their name, family, businesses, and ministries in the back of that year's journal. I am so glad I have done that, because even *that list reminds me* of all the ways *He has worked* mightily, *answered* completely, and *humbled* me as a result.

FATHER GOD often reveals amazing *insights* to me when I am reading the Bible, frequently *for those whose names are written in these journals.* For thirteen years, I have placed the journal, a black pen, and a red pen on the table next to where I read the Bible. When I tell you I will pray for you, your name goes into the back of the journal for that year. So when Charlie and I pray before going to bed, we include those listed in the back of my journals *all the way back* to when I was seventy years old. By faith, we join the hosts of heaven asking Him, in His Mercy and Grace, to hear the prayers we pray for all the people, their families, businesses and ministries. *One of our highest pleasures, JESUS, is to bring people before Your Throne!*

Beloved Reader and Participant in this Conversation in the Language of Heaven, you and I are coming to the end of our journey in this book GOD has written through me for you! I would humbly ask that you stop long enough to *consider where you are* with the *Five Gifts That Create Legacy.* Humbly, I thank GOD because He has loved us enough to give us a *Roadmap to Him. Be good* to yourself and to your descendants. *Find an extended time to invest with GOD in quiet places.* With gratitude and thanksgiving, *praise GOD for the reality* that He will always be there no matter what sacred time you choose to invite Him to join you.

I invite you to go to JESUS with unhindered honesty. Ask Him to show you where you stand with Him on a scale of 1-10 in each of the *Five Gifts That Create Legacy.* Ask Him to show you where to focus in the days to come. *Growing in each one will move you to strength in the next one.*

First, **INTIMACY**— Do you know GOD? Do you long to spend time in His Presence? Are you hungry and thirsty to read His Word? Do you seek to know what JESUS is praying for you? Do you enter His Presence with praise, thanksgiving and gratitude until you sense His Presence falling on you, then listen to hear a word, a phrase He gives you? Do you write to record your thanks to Him, and pray using those words ? Do you continue to pray that prayer until He answers it? When you pray, do you ever take enough time to know you are listening to GOD, joining GOD, or honoring GOD? Or do you just send a quick prayer up to Him and rush off to do "your stuff"?

Second, **IDENTITY**— Do you know what GOD calls you? Who does God say that you are? Have you asked GOD "What name did You write on my white stone? (Revelation 2:17) Do you walk in the names the world has given you or are you walking in the name that GOD created for you before the beginning of the world? (Psalm 139)

Third, **INTENT**—Do you know GOD'S Intended Purpose for your life? Have you asked Him why you were born? Are you walking in that purpose? Are you aware that the Cross represents only one thing for us—complete absolute perfect identification with the Lord JESUS Christ? Do you live by the truth that *there is nothing in which this identity is more real to us than in prayer?* When prayer seems to be unanswered, do you place the blame on someone else? (Oswald Chambers—My Utmost For His Highest)

Fourth, **INHERITANCE**—Are numbers 1,2, and 3 currently active in your life? Are you aware that your moment-by-moment words, thoughts and deeds are creating the future for your children, grandchildren, great grandchildren and your descendants for a thousand years forward or until Christ returns?

Fifth, **IMPACT**—Are FATHER GOD, JESUS, and HOLY SPIRIT your First Love? Do you love your neighbor as you have learned to love yourself with God's Pure Perfect Love? Are you aware that you have an ability to walk in humility; you have an ability to surrender totally to GOD; are you aware that you have the ability to receive GOD's wisdom, understanding, counsel, power, knowledge, and fear of the Lord ? Do you know that the answers to those questions impact positively or negatively your marriage, family and those around you for GOD'S Kingdom? Are *other people wondering why you are different? Do they know you love them? Do you serve more than you are served? Will heaven be more populated because you lived? Your First Love is the Key to your true significance and Impact* . . .

Friends, I don't know about you, but *I am humbled by these questions.* I don't fully measure up in most of them. But, this I can promise GOD: *He and I will spend much more time together* with me asking Him and listening to Him about how I can be better today on each of these *Five Gifts of Legacy* than I was yesterday. I will ask Him how I can be better tomorrow than I am today. I will be intentional about these gifts, for that shows the depth of the love I can activate for my family, my descendants, and all of you.!

I hope you will make that promise too. You and I will never regret it!

JESUS, as I talked to Kaelyn Benham today, I asked her a question, which for some people is an embarrassing one. I asked her "Kaelyn, how old are you?" She replied, "I am thirty eight years old". (Don't worry, I have gotten her permission to put her age here!) Then, I asked Kaelyn to give herself the gift of:

Pondering, in gratitude and thanksgiving how GOD has brought her these Five Gifts at the early age of thirty eight.

Remembering that if the LORD tarries—on her eighty-third birthday to stop, and humbly thank

FATHER GOD for His Kindness that He gave her the five gifts at the early age of thirty-eight. Thank Him for the wisdom He has given her each year from age thirty-eight until eighty-three to enrich the legacy she will leave her family, and the world!

Join Kaelyn by giving these two gifts to yourself as well!

JESUS, I thank You that, in Your Perfect Timing, You have now given to many others this Your Roadmap *soon enough that they can still live a LIFE of* Intimacy, Identity, Intent Inheritance and Impact! I want my ceiling to be your floor, so that no matter what your age you can be grateful GOD loves you so much! *I look forward to speaking* **THE LANGUAGE OF HEAVEN** with you in heaven.

BLESSING speaking to GOD as HOLY SPIRIT

HOLY SPIRIT, I sense You stirring once again a desire within me to declare the words of Ephesians 3:14-21 over each one reading this book, and their descendants for one thousand years forward or until JESUS comes. *There have been many times You have made this scripture stand out to me as I prayed over those who would read this book.*

In my imagination I am sitting with each reader declaring these words personally over each one of you. Please close your eyes and allow yourself to feel the PRESENCE OF GOD. After you rest in HIS PRESENCE awhile, open your eyes. Read these words, and imagine you hear my voice declaring these truths over you, and your descendants for a thousand years forward or until JESUS comes.

"My response is to get down on my knees before the FATHER, this magnificent FATHER Who parcels out all Heaven and Earth. I ask Him to strengthen you by His SPIRIT—not a brute strength, but a glorious inner strength- so that Christ will live in you as you open the door and invite Him in. And I ask Him that with both feet planted firmly on love, you'll be able to take in with all followers of JESUS, the extravagant dimensions of Christ's Love. Reach out and experience the breath! Test its length! Plumb the depths! Rise to the heights! Live full lives, full in the fullness of GOD. GOD can do anything, you know-far more than you could ever imagine or guess or request in your wildest dreams! He does it not by pushing us around, but by working within us, His SPIRIT deeply and gently within us. Glory to GOD in the church! Glory to GOD in the Messiah, in JESUS! Glory down all the generations! Glory through all millennia! Oh, yes!" *(Ephesians 3:14-21).*

The prayer you just prayed has gone before the Throne of GOD, and He is holding them in golden bowls full of incense, which are the prayers of GOD'S people for all generations. (Revelations 5:8 NIV)

Even so, LORD JESUS come!

Acknowledgments

Mark Williams—An Editor sent by God. This book is better since it has been touched by you. It received a polishing of clarity, beauty, and depth because of God's work through Mark.

Kary Oberbrunner & David Branderhorst—My publishers and my forever inspiration

Erica Foster—An unexpected blessing and partner whose book, "You Taught My Feet To Dance," has impacted and inspired scores of women and mothers in their lives and in their walk with GOD.

Melaney Massey—A giver of Heavenly gift. A GOD-appointed artist and painter of the front cover of **The Language of Heaven.**

About The Author

Pat is an author who seeks 'to watch with JESUS ' (Matt. 26:28). Yes, it requires identifying with JESUS through our own Gethsemane experiences, but the reward is a chance to live on earth as it is in heaven. It creates a oneness with the Creator of the universe that dispels darkness by His HOLY LIGHT.

Pat's first love is her heavenly family: FATHER GOD, JESUS, and HOLY SPIRIT. She began her walk with the supernatural encounter with JESUS at the age of three. She then questioned JESUS in college, forgot JESUS as she traveled the world seeking worldly values, sitting with JESUS in a church pew until she was seventy years old.

Something wonderful happened at that time! She humbled herself, surrendered all to JESUS for the privilege of 'watching with JESUS . . . expecting nothing, no agenda, just being with Him. Pat has been resting in

JESUS, listening to what GOD was doing and saying for thirteen years now. Guided by the HOLY SPIRIT, these thirteen years Pat is learning to live Kingdom living on earth.

Pat's second love on earth is her family. It is through her blessed marriage, her beloved children, and their families that GOD has taught her the value of family. Even though each of us has experienced deep sorrow, it is through those very things that GOD has shown Pat His truth that the depth of pain, which is the enemy's plan, is the height of beauty of GOD'S CALLING. A truth that Pat now teaches as others go through their own valleys.

GOD has shown Pat, her family, and others that under the shield of GOD'S wings is a sweet, calm loving place of transformation. Pat is passionate to build a new kind of army that encourages everyone, no matter what age, to recognize that life is a beautiful staircase. It is our privilege to go up higher year by year. We would get wiser, would give more, would be more thankful, would sing more, would lie under the stars more, and we would be more grateful. More importantly we would love more deeply, more sacrificially than we did last year and definitely less than we will next year.

Pat is a John Maxwell certified Life Coach, Trainer, and Speaker. She is CEO Of Freeing Souls To Soar, and she is a member of the Igniting Souls Tribe. She is an author with Kary Oberbrunner and David Branderhorst as her publishers.

Contact Pat

Email
ganopat@columbus.rr.com

Or visit her website at
patgano.com

You may also find her on Facebook
@patganoauthor

CPSIA information can be obtained
at www.ICGtesting.com
Printed in the USA
LVOW10s1442061217
558849LV00020B/222/P